Con *dren*

UIDE

413

Conversational Spanish
for Children

A CURRICULUM GUIDE

MARCIA HARMON ROSENBUSCH

ANA MARÍA R. GRABER

Iowa State University Press / AMES

MARCIA HARMON ROSENBUSCH, holds an M.S. degree in child development and has taught child development and Spanish at college and elementary school levels.

ANA MARÍA R. GRABER taught beginning, intermediate, and conversational Spanish at preschool, elementary school, and adult levels.

Cover photograph by **Barbara Spike**

© 1982 The Iowa State University Press. All rights reserved

Printed by The Iowa State University Press, Ames, Iowa 50010

First edition, 1982

International Standard Book Number: 0-8138-0336-5
Library of Congress Catalog Card Number: 81-85749

Contents

Preface

The tremendous surge in foreign language programs in the elementary schools (FLES), which began in the 1950s with the introduction of the audio-lingual method, has weakened in the last ten years. Yet, even though FLES programs are not currently the focus of attention of foreign language educators, these programs continue to exist in elementary schools throughout the nation. At some schools the foreign language program is part of the regular elementary school curriculum and at others it is extracurricular. The extracurricular programs are often organized and administered by parents who are convinced that their children should receive foreign language instruction during the grade school years.

There have been no lines of communication among these programs on a national level, and a listing of the schools that offer FLES programs is not readily available. However, the desire to communicate with other FLES teachers and to share and compare experiences exists; when presentations on FLES have been made at workshops, FLES educators are eager to talk with each other about their experiences in teaching foreign languages at the elementary school level.

FLES teachers often develop their own materials and programs because they have found that the available teaching materials do not satisfy their own nor their children's needs. For that reason this curriculum was developed. It is shared now as a means of stimulating thinking about teaching children a foreign language and to offer a framework around which to build a program.

Although this curriculum is presented for the Spanish language, it has been adapted to French, German, and English as a second language with equal success. Since the methodology is child oriented, with adaptations made to allow for the differences between languages, it works equally well in the teaching of any second language to children. Using the same basic methodology in teaching all the second languages offered within a school is advantageous because a stronger, more unified program results. To make these ideas accessible to teachers of other languages and to administrators, the Spanish has been translated to English throughout most of the guide.

This curriculum is meant to be used as a reference by teachers in the planning and teaching of their classroom program. It is essential to the success of the program that the teachers have good speaking skill in the language. The goal of this curriculum is to teach children the skills necessary for participation in conversation--the informal, spontaneous exchange of thoughts and feelings. The teaching of reading and writing are not within its scope; it is advantageous to teach these skills after the skill of speaking has been well established.

vii

This curriculum focuses on the organization of grammatical content and suggests methodology to be used in teaching grammatical concepts. This material can be used, together with songs, games, and cultural information, to develop a total classroom program that responds to each particular teaching situation.

This material can be used in programs that differ from one another in several aspects--for example, the length of class meeting time; the number of days the class meets each week; the size of the class; and the grade level of students, whether mixed or from one grade. A primary concern in developing this curriculum has been to make the organization of the material flexible enough for it to be adapted easily to each teaching situation. To provide for this, the grammatical content has been organized into an outline consisting of six levels that may parallel grades one through six or be used with other kinds of group organization. For example, children of any age beginning the study of the language would begin with Level 1. If the presentation is adapted to the interests of older children, they respond as enthusiastically as the younger ones. A section on planning is included to help teachers develop a program that responds to the needs of their individual teaching situations.

The basic methodology of this curriculum is a concrete-action approach such as is currently used in elementary schools throughout the nation. The children have direct contact with materials that represent the vocabulary being studied and participate actively and physically in the classroom. There is also emphasis on the stimulation of the children's creativity, especially in the later levels of the curriculum in which their ideas are used in developing dialogues and conversations. The utilization of the children's creativity in the foreign language classes makes good sense, for children are more eager to learn to say what they want to than what an adult might consider to be of interest to them.

The material presented has been selected and organized to make learning to speak a second language a manageable task for children. The language presented proceeds from the simple to the complex. Children learn the basic syntactical structures by imitation and then learn to substitute other words into those structures, creating their own sentences. Gradually they are introduced to more complex structures.

After Level 1, in which the imperative is used for reasons described in detail, the present tense of the indicative is the only verb form taught. The number of tenses introduced to the children has been limited so that they can learn the present tense well, providing a solid basis for study of other tenses in the future. The present tense allows for greater possibilities for expression than any other individual verb tense.

Each of the six levels focuses on a particular person of the verb. Extensive practice is provided in the use of that person so that children can master its use. The methodology used is related to the person of the verb taught and to the children's growing ability to use the language. A summary of the verb forms and the methodology emphasized in each level is included here.

	VERB FORM EMPHASIZED	BASIC METHODOLOGY
	Imperative	
Level 1:	Second person singular (s.), intimate (int.)	Commands
	Indicative	
Level 2:	First person singular	Descriptions

Level 3:	Third person singular	Descriptions
Level 4:	Second person singular, intimate and formal (for.)	Dialogues and conversations
Level 5:	First and third persons plural (pl.); second person plural, formal	Dialogues and conversations
Level 6:	First, second, and third persons singular of reflexive verbs; review of all verb forms	Dialogues and conversations

Each level consists of (1) an introduction that includes a discussion of the general methodology, (2) a discussion of the selection and use of the vocabulary and examples of usage (Los Verbos [Verbs], Oraciones Interrogativas [Interrogative Sentences], Expresiones Comunes [Common Expressions], Vocabulario Suplementario [Supplementary Vocabulary], Vocabulario Básico [Basic Vocabulary]), and (3) a listing of the vocabulary introduced.

The vocabulary is organized into verbs; the basic vocabulary areas, e.g., foods, animals; interrogative sentences; common expressions; and supplementary vocabulary, e.g., adjectives, adverbs. The number of words included in each level has been kept to a minimum so that children are able to master them and to allow the teacher to add additional words according to the interests and needs of the particular group. Every effort has been made to select Spanish vocabulary that is internationally accepted instead of words that represent a particular region or country. The vocabulary contains words that are of interest to children of this country, such as gloves, pancakes, even though they might not refer to objects common in all Spanish speaking countries.

While the concern of this curriculum is program content, other aspects of FLES programs need careful consideration by foreign language educators; for example, the preparation of FLES teachers, techniques for evaluating student progress, individualized instruction, and research in the area of FLES. Increased communication at the regional and national levels among FLES educators would be valuable in stimulating thinking about these aspects and would be likely to give new impetus to the teaching of foreign languages.

We wish to thank Carolyn Jons, former Chairperson of the Ames Foreign Language Association, and Glenn Connor, principal, Northwood Elementary School, who supported the development of this curriculum guide. They encouraged the authors to test and implement many of the ideas in this book in the Ames Program.

We thank Dr. Arturo Graupera for his helpful suggestions and careful review of the manuscript and Dr. Walter L. Chatfield for his early and continuing support for the project.

Conversational Spanish for Children

A CURRICULUM GUIDE

LEVEL 1

A critical period in teaching children a second language is their first contact with the language. The attitudes developed at this time color significantly their feelings toward the study of a second language and toward themselves as language learners. It is essential that the children's first experience with the language be positive.

The material taught should be challenging but not overwhelming. Simple syntax and ease of pronunciation need to characterize the material first presented. The amount taught must be limited, for children need time to learn new material thoroughly and review it often. When the material has been absorbed, the children will use it confidently and will feel successful.

The material taught should be meaningful to children. It should demonstrate to them that the second language is as vital and workable as their own and that with it they can express things that are important to them. They need to experience communication with others in the second language; they need to see concrete results from their communication.

The material and methodology of this level have been carefully chosen to help ensure children a positive first experience. A concrete-action approach is used in which the vocabulary words are represented concretely with teaching materials, and action verbs allow children to act out verbalizations.

The action verbs are introduced in the imperative or command form in the first level. Five commands are introduced:

1. Pásame (pass [to] me) is a favorite command because it allows children to choose from a group of objects the one they want to hold and explore firsthand:
Pásame el avión, por favor. (Pass me the airplane, please.)

2. Tírame (throw [to] me) is used with any object that will not break if it falls or hurt children as they catch it:
Tírame la pelota, por favor. (Throw me the ball, please.)

3. Toca (touch) can be used with any type of teaching material:
Toca el árbol, por favor. (Touch the tree, please.)

4 and 5. Pon (put on) and saca (remove) are used with the flannel board and stick-on figures:
Pon la casa, por favor. (Put on the house, please.)
Saca el perro, por favor. (Remove the dog, please.)

There are important reasons for using the command form of action verbs

3

with children who are just beginning the study of a second language. From
the time that a command and several vocabulary words are learned, the children can communicate directly with each other. They have concrete evidence
that the second language "works" when their companions respond physically to
their commands.

Children have a tremendous amount of physical energy and find it difficult to sit quietly in the classroom. By requiring their physical participation in the activities, action verb commands enable children to use their en-
ergies in a positive way.

The use of commands allows children to touch and hold the teaching materials that the vocabulary words represent. Grade school children are still
close to the time when as infants they first learned about objects and the
relationships between objects by experiencing and experimenting with them directly. Children still are pleased to hold objects that attract their attention and find this aspect of using commands especially enjoyable.

The most important advantage of this methodology is that the use of commands permits children to create sentences to express their own ideas. For
example, when one command, such as pásame (pass [to] me), is used with several nouns that represent objects, such as cat, ball, dog, apple, or car, the
child decides which object to ask for and creates a sentence: Pásame el gato,
por favor. (Pass me the cat, please.) Later, when several commands have
been learned, the child can decide what might be done with which object and
create a sentence to express it: Tírame la pelota, por favor. (Throw me the
ball, please.) Toca el perro, por favor. (Touch the dog, please.)

Thus the commands enable children to express sentences of their own from
the beginning of their study. They provide children with valuable practice
in making sentences, a skill that is essential to conversation. With the
commands children also have the pleasure of deciding what they want to say
instead of repeating by rote that which the adult dictates.

This methodology has advantages for the teachers also. The use of commands allows the teacher to evaluate easily a child's comprehension of the
second language. For example, a child who is asked to touch the banana and
touches the apple instead or passes the banana instead of touching it does not
yet recognize the words for "touch" and "banana." When children respond correctly to a command they give a clear demonstration of their comprehension of
the language.

Teachers find that numerous possibilities for variety are provided in the
activities. A single vocabulary word, such as la flor (flower) can be reviewed by using several different representations of the flower: a flash
card, a flannel or a paper cutout, a plastic or a real flower. These five
representations can be used with all five commands: pass [to] me, throw [to]
me, touch, put on, and remove. Multiplying the number of possible representations of the word by the five commands, it is evident that the word la flor
(flower) can be reviewed on twenty-five consecutive days without repeating the
same activity. Children delight in this variety and interest remains high
throughout the frequent review necessary for mastering the material.

It is essential to understand clearly the teacher's role in this methodology. The children speak during the greater part of the class time for they
are the ones who need practice in the use of the language. The teacher's role
is that of planning, organizing, and directing activities.

In planning, the teacher decides which vocabulary and teaching materials
to use and how the activities will be carried out. The teacher introduces the
activity and helps to start it, oversees it, clarifies misunderstandings and
redefines limits when necessary, and brings it to a close. The children are

the participants in the activity, communicating directly with each other and handling the teaching materials themselves.

In introducing new vocabulary and whenever necessary for further clarification, the teacher serves as a model for the children. A word is introduced with an object that it represents. For example, la manzana (apple) might be taught using a real apple. The teacher says the word la manzana while the children explore the apple: seeing, feeling, smelling, and perhaps tasting. As the sound of the word becomes familiar to them, they imitate the teacher in saying la manzana. When the children are able to say the word easily, the teacher models the use of the word with a command, for example: María, pásame la manzana, por favor. (Mary, pass me the apple, please.) When the children have heard the command, can respond correctly to it, and can repeat it easily, they are ready to use the command with each other. The children are eager to handle the apple and are thus motivated to learn the new word and use it in a command.

Masculine (m.) and feminine (f.) vocabulary words are introduced together in this level, reflecting the reality of the Spanish language. The corresponding article is always used with the word so that children will become aware of the existence of la (feminine) and el (masculine) words. This understanding is essential for making correct noun-adjective agreement. To ensure that children develop the necessary awareness of the two kinds of nouns, the teacher can have the children separate the objects or flash cards into two piles, the la words and the el words.

When children have learned to use the commands with the vocabulary words and are aware of feminine and masculine words, the plural and the color adjectives can be introduced. To avoid confusion it is important that the plural and the adjectives not be used together until each has been mastered individually. (The methodology suggested for teaching the plural and the adjectives is discussed in the next section.)

The vocabulary presented in this level has been kept to a minimum for two reasons: (1) Children should have time to learn the vocabulary and basic syntactic structures thoroughly to provide a solid foundation for their study, and (2) young children need an especially varied and active class time. Regular class activities need to be interspersed with change-of-pace activities such as songs and games and with cultural information. If time permits, additional words of special interest to the group can be taught.

Ease of pronunciation is an important consideration in the vocabulary of this level. Diphthongs have been avoided and words with few syllables have been chosen. The vocabulary selected represents objects and situations that are of interest to young children--family, pets, and friends.

Since rote conjugation of verbs is not taught, it is not necessary to limit verbs to those that are conjugated regularly. One irregular verb is included in the first level: poner (to put); and two orthographic-changing verbs are included: sacar (to remove) and tocar (to touch).

S E L E C T I O N   A N D   U S E   O F   V O C A B U L A R Y

Los Verbos (Verbs)
The commands used in Level 1 are in the intimate of the second person singular. This verb form has been chosen because the intimate is the correct form to use with and among children. In Level 4, children learn to use the second person formal and to distinguish between the usage of the intimate and the formal.

As the children learn the commands, they need to realize that these commands are said by a child to another child or by a child to an adult who is a family member or good friend. They must understand that these commands are not used with other adults. If the children want to use these commands with their teacher, they need to pretend that the teacher is a child. They will enjoy this tremendously and it will help them remember that later they will learn a different way of addressing their teacher and other adults.

In addition to the commands already discussed, two verbs are introduced in Level 1 in the first person singular of the indicative: me llamo (my name is) and vivo (I live). They are used to answer the two interrogative sentences taught in this level and to preview the extensive use of the first person singular in Level 2.

Oraciones Interrogativas (Interrogative Sentences)

An important aspect of this methodology is that the question-answer pattern is not used extensively with beginning students. It is difficult for children new to the study of a language to change the person of the verb used in the question to that used in the answer. With the command-physical response pattern meaningful communication can occur without a change in the verb form.

The ability to use questions is important in Level 4 when the children begin creating dialogues and conversations. To prepare for this, asking and answering questions is taught gradually. Several interrogative sentences are taught in each level.

In this level, two questions are taught. First the teacher models the use of a question and answer, perhaps with the use of puppets. The answer is practiced with the group; then the question is asked of individuals. When they are able to answer the question easily, they are taught how to form the question and can begin using the question with each other. Using a puppet can help children feel more at ease in asking and answering questions. Since the questions are taught in the intimate of the second person singular, the children do not use them with the teacher unless the teacher pretends to be a child.

The first question taught is: ¿Cómo te llamas? (What is your name?) The children answer: Me llamo (María). (My name is [Mary].) The second question taught has several possible answers: ¿Dónde vives? (Where do you live?) Vivo en (Chicago). (I live in [Chicago].) Vivo en (Illinois). (I live in [Illinois].) Vivo en (los Estados Unidos). (I live in [the United States].)

Espresiones Comunes (Common Expressions)

The greetings buenos días (good morning) and adíos (good-bye) are taught in this level. If the class meets in the afternoon, buenas tardes (good afternoon) should be taught instead of buenos días. Besides using these as greetings in the classroom they may be used in short dialogues in which the children greet each other or a puppet and ask and answer the questions they have learned.

Several polite expressions are taught and used with the commands. The children delight in making sure that the polite expressions are added; for example, they will not complete the action required by the command until "please" is added. The following illustration clarifies the usage of the polite expressions.

Gloria: Jorge, pásame el árbol, por favor. (George, pass me the tree, please.)

Gloria, as George passes the tree to her: Gracias. (Thank you.)
Jorge: De nada. (You're welcome.)

Either repite, por favor (please repeat) or perdón (pardon) is used when the children need to have a command or question repeated.

Vocabulario Suplementario (Supplementary Vocabulary)

en (in). This preposition is used with the verb vivo (I live) in indicating where one lives: Vivo en (Chicago, Illinois). (I live in [Chicago, Illinois].)

señor, señora, señorita (Mr., Mrs., Miss). The appropriate term is used when the children address their teacher.

la pelota (ball). This object is a favorite to be used with the command tírame (throw [to] me). (A very soft ball that is not bouncy is the best kind to use in the classroom.) Tírame la pelota, por favor. (Throw me the ball, please.)

Los Números (Numbers)

Some children will have learned to count in Spanish from watching children's television programs that teach some Spanish words. Therefore it is best to begin the study of numbers with counting. When the children can count to ten, they need to practice recognizing the numbers out of order. To help children learn this, the numbers can be written on flash cards or can be prepared as flannel cutouts. These numbers can be used as objects and handled in response to commands, for example:

Pásame el número cinco, por favor. (Pass me the number five, please.)
Pon el número siete, por favor. (Put on the number seven, please.)

When the numbers are recognized out of order, the plural can be taught. Since the formation of the plural is similar to the formation of the plural in English, children usually have little difficulty with it. The numbers can be used with the teaching materials to teach the plural of the nouns. To avoid extensive duplication of objects, the children can imagine that the number laid next to an object magically transforms that object into the quantity of objects indicated by the number, for example:

Pásame seis piñas, por favor. (Pass me six pineapples, please.)
Toca diez gatos, por favor. (Touch ten cats, please.)

Las and los, the plurals of the articles la and el (the--f., m.) can be taught with several series of similar objects; for example:

Pon los aviones, por favor. (Put on the airplanes, please.)
Saca las manzanas, por favor. (Remove the apples, please.)

Los Colores (Colors)

To teach the names of the colors, individual flash cards or flannel cutouts for each color that allow children to focus on the color only can be used. Sentences can be formed and the color objects handled as with objects represented by other vocabulary words. For example:

Pásame el color rojo, por favor. (Pass me the red color, please.)

Toca el color negro, por favor.   (Touch the black color, please.)

When colors are taught in this way, children learn the color words and at the same time become acquainted with the positioning of these words in sentences.
When first used as adjectives with nouns, it is helpful to use the color names to modify only masculine nouns so that children can practice the positioning of the adjective without having to focus on the agreement necessary with feminine nouns:

Saca el avión rojo, por favor.   (Remove the red airplane, please.)
Tírame el perro negro, por favor.   (Throw me the black dog, please.)

As with numbers, to avoid duplication of the teaching materials the children can pretend that an object transforms itself into the color next to which it is placed; for example, when the red flower is placed on the white flash card, the flower becomes white. Children have good imaginations and enjoy pretending that the color has changed.
When children are able to position the color adjectives without difficulty, the adjectives should be used extensively with feminine nouns so that the change in the adjective necessary when modifying feminine nouns becomes automatic. In this level, the three color adjectives all require a change when used with feminine nouns:

Toca la casa roja.   (Touch the red house.)
Pon la boca blanca.   (Put on the white mouth).

It is wise to provide extensive practice in the use of adjectives in this level, for without the ability to use adjectives children are limited in what they can express in their sentences.

Los Colores y Los Números (Colors and Numbers Used Together)
Since the plural is less difficult to learn than the use of adjectives it is suggested that the plural be taught first; then the use of adjectives; and last, the combination of plural and adjectives. When teaching the use of the plural with adjectives, it is helpful to retrace the steps used in teaching noun-adjective agreement in the singular; i.e., begin with masculine nouns and follow with feminine nouns. If the usage of colors and numbers has been well learned separately, their use together will be easier. For example:

Saca cuatro gatos blancos, por favor.   (Remove four white cats, please.)
Pásame siete flores rojas, por favor.   (Pass me seven red flowers, please.)

Vocabulario Básico (Basic Vocabulary)
This section illustrates how the nouns of the remaining basic vocabulary areas, the verbs, and the adjectives or modifiers can be used together to form sentences. Teaching materials are listed with each verb to suggest which materials can be used when that verb is combined with the nouns. The sentence variations that result from the combination of these elements are too numerous to list, but several examples are included. The sentences have been selected to demonstrate varying levels of skill in vocabulary use. For translation of vocabulary, see Appendix D.

Los alimentos (Foods)

Nouns	Verbs	Teaching materials	Modifiers
la manzana	pásame	real objects, toys,	blanco, negro, rojo
la piña		flash cards, cutouts	1-10
el plátano		of flannel or paper	
	pon, saca	cutouts of flannel	
		or paper	
	tírame	toys, flash cards,	
		cutouts of flannel	
	toca	all above materials	

Examples of sentences
Tírame la piña, por favor. (Throw me the pineapple, please.)
Pásame tres plátanos, por favor. (Pass me three bananas, please.)
Pon la manzana roja, por favor. (Put on the red apple, please.)

Los animales (Animals)

Nouns	Verbs	Teaching materials	Modifiers
el gato	pásame	real animals, toys,	blanco, negro, rojo
el perro		flash cards, cutouts	1-10
		of flannel or paper	
	pon, saca	cutouts of flannel	
		or paper	
	tírame	soft toys, flash	
		cards, cutouts of	
		flannel	
	toca	all above materials	

Examples of sentences
Pásame el perro, por favor. (Pass me the dog, please.)
Saca ocho perros, por favor. (Remove eight dogs, please.)
Toca el gato negro, por favor. (Touch the black cat, please.)

La casa (House)

Nouns	Verbs	Teaching materials	Modifiers
la casa	pásame	toys, flash cards,	blanco, negro, rojo
		cutouts of flannel	1-10
		or paper	
	pon, saca	cutouts of flannel	
		or paper	
	tírame	soft toys, flash cards,	
		cutouts of flannel	
	toca	all above materials	

Examples of sentences
Tírame la casa roja, por favor. (Throw me the red house, please.)
Pon dos casas, por favor. (Put on two houses, please.)
Toca tres casas blancas, por favor. (Touch three white houses, please.)

El cuerpo humano (Body parts)

Nouns	Verbs	Teaching materials	Modifiers
la boca	pásame	flash cards, cutouts	blanco, negro, rojo
la cabeza		of flannel or paper	1-10
la mano	pon, saca	cutouts of flannel	
la nariz		or paper	
el ojo	tírame	flash cards, cutouts	
el pelo		of flannel	
	toca	their own body parts,	
		toys, and all above	
		materials	

Examples of sentences

Pásame la boca, por favor. (Pass me the mouth, please.)
Pon dos ojos, por favor. (Put on two eyes, please.)
Tírame la nariz roja, por favor.   (Throw me the red nose, please.)

La familia (Family)

Nouns	Verbs	Teaching materials	Modifiers
la mamá	pásame	dolls, puppets, flash	blanco, negro, rojo
la niña		cards, cutouts of	1-10
el niño		flannel or paper	
el papá	pon, saca	cutouts of flannel or	
		paper	
	tírame	soft dolls, puppets,	
		flash cards, flannel	
		cutouts	
	toca	all above materials	

Examples of sentences

Toca la mamá, por favor. (Touch the mom, please.)
Saca dos niñas, por favor. (Remove two girls, please.)
Pon el papá negro, por favor. (Put on the black dad, please.)

La naturaleza (Nature)

Nouns	Verbs	Teaching materials	Modifiers
el árbol	pásame	real objects, toys,	blanco, negro, rojo
la flor		flash cards, cutouts	1-10
		of flannel or paper	
	pon, saca	cutouts of flannel	
		or paper	
	tírame	real objects, soft	
		toys, flash cards,	
		cutouts of flannel	
	toca	all above materials	

Examples of sentences

Tírame la flor, por favor. (Throw me the flower, please.)
Pásame cinco árboles, por favor. (Pass me five trees, please.)
Toca tres flores rojas, por favor. (Touch three red flowers, please.)

Transporte (Transportation)

Nouns	Verbs	Teaching materials	Modifiers
el automóvil	pásame	toys, flash cards, cutouts of flannel or paper	blanco, negro, rojo
el avión			1-10
	pon, saca	cutouts of flannel or paper	
	tírame	soft toys, flash cards, cutouts of flannel	
	toca	all above materials	

Examples of sentences
Pon el avión, por favor. (Put on the airplane, please.)
Saca el automóvil negro, por favor. (Remove the black car, please.)
Pásame tres aviones blancos, por favor. (Pass me three white airplanes, please.)

VOCABULARY

Los Verbos
me llamo
pásame*
pon*
saca*
tírame*
toca*
vivo

Vocabulario Básico

Los alimentos
la manzana
la piña
el plátano

Los animales
el gato
el perro

La casa
la casa

Los colores
el color
blanco
negro
rojo

El cuerpo humano
la boca
la cabeza
la mano
la nariz
el ojo
el pelo

La familia
la mamá
la niña
el niño
el papá

La naturaleza
el árbol
la flor

Los números
el número
1-10

Transporte
el automóvil
el avión

---

*Command form of the verb.

Oraciones Interrogativas
¿Cómo te llamas?
¿Dónde vives?

Expresiones Comunes
adiós
buenos días
de nada
gracias
perdón
por favor
repite

Vocabulario Suplementario
en
señor
señora
señorita
la pelota

LEVEL 2

In Level 2 the verb form emphasized is the first person singular of the indicative. This verb form can be introduced by teaching children to respond verbally as well as physically to the commands they learned in the previous level. For example:

Gloria: María, pásame la piña, por favor. (Mary, pass me the pineapple, please.)
María, as she passes the pineapple to Gloria: Paso la piña a Gloria. (I pass the pineapple to Gloria.)

It is helpful to limit the use of the first person singular to sentences employing the already familiar nouns of Level 1 until this new verb form is learned well. Later when new nouns of this level are introduced, they are first employed in sentences using this command, first person singular exchange. This pattern is used with new nouns throughout the remaining levels. Children enjoy handling the objects represented by nouns while they respond verbally to a command, and their learning is reinforced by physical contact with the object.

Self-description is another way in which the first person singular is used. In this level, children begin to create self-descriptions. The children decide what they want to say about themselves, form sentences using the basic syntactical structures learned, and combine the sentences in their own way. For example:

Me llamo Juan. (My name is John.)
Tengo ocho años. (I am eight years old.)
Amo a mis abuelos. (I love my grandparents.)
Ayudo a mi profesor. (I help my teacher.)
Llevo puesta una camisa nueva. (I am wearing a new shirt.)
Tengo hambre y sed. (I am hungry and thirsty.)
Me gustan el cereal y la leche. (I like cereal and milk.)
Me duelen los dedos, pero no me duelen las manos. (My fingers hurt, but my hands don't hurt.)
No tengo ni un gato ni un perro. (I don't have a cat or a dog.)

The descriptions developed in this level are important in Level 3 when children use the third person singular to describe their companions and base those descriptions on what they have heard in this level.

Descriptions of what can be seen in the classroom or in illustrations are

13

also introduced in Level 2. The verb forms <u>veo</u> (I see) and <u>hay</u> (there is, there are) are useful in making these descriptions. They can be guided at first by the teacher: ¿Qué ves? (What do you see?) ¿Qué más ves? (What else do you see?) ¿Cuántos ——— hay? (How many ——— are there?) When the children are familiar with these questions they can take turns asking them of each other, gaining practice in the use of questions.

Many variations of describing what they see can be used. For example, the teacher or a child can select certain familiar objects and place them together for the children to see. The children close their eyes as several objects are removed. When they open their eyes, one of them states which objects are missing:

No veo ni el caballo, ni el cerdo, ni la vaca. (I don't see the horse, or the pig, or the cow.)

Because children are naturally creative and have excellent imaginations, they like to pretend that they are in a given situation and describe what they see, do, and feel. The teaching materials can be used to help stimulate the children's imaginations. In the following example, a child is pretending to be at the breakfast table:

Tengo hambre. (I'm hungry.)
Veo el cereal, la leche, el jugo de piña y las tostadas. (I see the cereal, the milk, the pineapple juice, and the toast.)
No me gusta el jugo de piña. (I don't like pineapple juice.)
No bebo el jugo. (I don't drink the juice.)
Como una tostada y bebo la leche. (I eat a piece of toast and drink the milk.)

In such descriptions, children should be encouraged to dramatize the actions and feelings that they are describing. They enjoy transmitting the message physically as well as verbally and dramatization will confirm the meaning of the message.

When children begin to make descriptions, they will want to use words that are not part of their vocabulary yet. This situation is common to all students when they first try to communicate in the language they are learning. The teacher can expand the children's vocabulary to include new words, but an important skill that language students must develop is that of learning to express themselves within the limits of their vocabulary. If they depend on others to fill in missing words or if they wait to speak until they know all the vocabulary they will need in every situation, they will never learn to communicate in the second language. Children need to understand this situation and should be encouraged to communicate all that they can with the vocabulary that they have learned.

In this level the children learn to make longer, more detailed sentences with the introduction of conjunctions and adverbs and the addition of adjectives. Their possibilities for expression are also increased by the introduction of the negative. The use of these new elements is illustrated in Vocabulario Suplementario (Supplementary Vocabulary).

SELECTION   AND   USE   OF   VOCABULARY

Los Verbos (Verbs)
Besides the first person singular of the commands taught in Level 1, sev-

eral new commands and corresponding first person singular forms are taught in
this level. The commands are first practiced alone. When the children use
them easily, the first person singular is taught and used with the command.
(Asterisk denotes the command form of the verb.)

abre,* abro (open, I open); cierra,* cierro (close, I close). These
verbs can be used with body parts: la boca (mouth), las manos (hands), and
los ojos (eyes), and with la ventana (window) and la puerta (door).
   Cierra la puerta, por favor. (Close the door, please.)
   Abro las manos. (I open my hands.)

camina,* camino (walk, I walk; corre,* corro (run, I run); salta,* salto
(jump, I jump). Because these verbs require children to be active they make
a good change of pace from the quieter activities. Used with the preposition
hacia (toward) and with objects, person's names, or the stressed pronoun mí
(me), these verbs indicate how children should move or are moving toward some-
thing or someone.
   Corre hacia la puerta. (Run toward the door.)
   Salto hacia Jorge. (I jump toward George.)
   Camina hacia mí. (Walk toward me.)

dibuja,* dibujo (draw, I draw). This verb is helpful for reviewing vocabulary; children can draw a face, reviewing the parts learned; or they can
draw a scene reviewing other vocabulary, such as house, animals, family, and
school. Children can take turns giving commands to their companions and can
cooperate in drawing the scene. Children like to draw objects in an exaggerated way, making a funny picture, especially when drawing a face.
   Dibuja una nariz fea. (Draw an ugly nose.)
   Dibujo dos ojos cerrados. (I draw two closed eyes.)

Suggestions are included for the usage of the other new verbs in this
level.

ayudo (I help); amo (I love). Both of these verbs require the personal
a when used with a direct object that refers to a specific person.
   Ayudo a mi mamá. (I help my mom.)
   Amo a mi abuelo. (I love my grandfather.)

como (I eat); bebo (I drink). These actions are especially good for
dramatization and combine well with the command pásame (pass [to] me).

   Pásame el pan, por favor. Como el pan. (Pass me the bread, please. I eat
the bread.)

gusta, gustan (pleases, please); duele, duelen (hurts, hurt). These
verbs are used with the indirect object pronoun me (to me). As is common, me
gusta is translated here to "I like" instead of "pleases me," which is the
literal translation.
   Me duele el brazo. (My arm hurts.)
   Me duelen las manos. (My hands hurt.)
   Me gusta la falda marrón. (I like the brown skirt.)
   Me gustan los zapatos nuevos. (I like the new shoes.)

llevo puesto (I am wearing)

---

*
 Command form of the verb.

Llevo puesta una blusa roja. (I am wearing a red blouse.)

   soy (I am)
Soy una niña. (I am a girl.)
Soy la amiga de Gloria. (I am Gloria's friend.)
Soy la gallina. (I am the chicken.) (Used in dramatizing songs, etc.)

   tengo (I have). This verb is also used with several idioms introduced in
this level and discussed in Vocabulario Suplementario (Supplementary Vocabulary).
Tengo el tractor. (I have the tractor.)
Tengo un perro y dos gatos. (I have a dog and two cats.)

   veo (I see); hay (there is, there are)
Veo el aula. (I see the classroom.)
Hay quince alumnos en el aula. (There are fifteen students in the class-
room.)

   voy (I go); regreso (I return)
Voy a la escuela. (I am going to school.)
Regreso a mi casa ahora. (I am returning to my house now.)

Oraciones Interrogativas (Interrogative Sentences)
     The interrogative sentences of this level are introduced and used in the
same way as those of Level 1. A common question asked of children is taught:
¿Cuántos años tienes? (How old are you?) The answer to this question is also
incorporated into the descriptions the children make of themselves; for example: Tengo (ocho) años. (I am [eight] years old.)
     The questions ¿Cuántos ——— hay? (How many ——— is/are there?) and
¿Qué ves? (What do you see?) are useful in asking children to describe what
they see in illustrations or in the classroom.
     A question that is helpful in reviewing body parts is: ¿Dónde te duele?
(Where do you hurt?) Since the answer may use either the singular or the
plural form of the verb, children are introduced to the change necessary when
using the plural: Me duele el dedo. (My finger hurts.) Me duelen los dedos.
(My fingers hurt.)

Expresiones Comunes (Common Expressions)
     The farewell hasta luego (until later) is introduced here and can be used
as an alternative to adiós (good-bye) of Level 1. Two more expressions of
greeting are also taught: buenas tardes (good afternoon) and buenas noches
(good night).
     To practice the correct use of the greetings, children will need to imag-
ine that it is morning, afternoon, or evening. A flash card with a sun that
is just rising can be used to symbolize morning. A full sun can be made to
symbolize afternoon and a moon can symbolize evening. Children will use the
expression of greeting appropriate for the flash card that is being displayed
at the moment.

Vocabulario Suplementario (Supplementary Vocabulary)
     yo (I, subject pronoun). In Spanish the subject pronoun of the first
person singular is not used except for emphasis. The children first learn to
use the first person singular verb form without the subject pronoun, then
learn to add it for emphasis.

¡Yo no soy el profesor, yo soy el alumno! (I'm not the professor, I'm the student!)

mi, mis (my--s., pl.). The possessive adjective is useful in the descriptions the children make about themselves.
Amo a mi papá. (I love my dad.)
Amo a mis abuelos. (I love my grandparents.)

me (to me). This pronoun is used as an indirect object with the verbs gustar (to please) and doler (to hurt).
Me gusta el cereal. (I like the cereal.)
Me duelen los ojos. (My eyes hurt.)

mí (me). The stressed object pronoun is used as the object of the prepositions hacia (toward) and a (to).
Camina hacia mí, por favor. (Walk toward me, please.)
A mí me gustan los cerdos. (I like pigs.)

un, una (a, an--m., f.); unos, unas (some--m., f.). The indefinite article can be taught with several objects of one category to which reference is made.
Pásame un animal, por favor. (Pass me an animal, please.)
Tírame unas flores, por favor. (Throw me some flowers, please.)
It can also be used in describing what the children see in a group of objects or in an illustration.
Veo un árbol, una flor y un perro. (I see a tree, a flower, and a dog.)

a, al, a la (to). The use of this preposition can be learned by the children through modeling. Several kinds of sentences are used in this level that require this preposition--statements made by the children as they complete an action that involves another person, description of feelings toward another person, and sentences using verbs of motion. Examples are, respectively:
Paso la oveja a Jorge. (I pass the sheep to George.)
Amo a mi mamá. (I love my mom.)
Regreso al aula. (I am returning to the classroom.)
Voy a la escuela. (I am going to school.)

sí (yes); no (no). These adverbs are taught as children learn to make negative as well as affirmative statements. Negative commands are not used.
No, no voy a la casa de mi abuela. (No, I'm not going to my grandmother's house.)
Sí, veo trece gatos. (Yes, I see thirteen cats.)

y (and); o (either, or); ni (neither, nor); pero (but). The conjunctions permit children to make longer sentences while avoiding complex sentence construction. The conjunction pero (but) is useful in practicing the negative by contrasting affirmative and negative statements.
Toco el gato, el perro, la oveja y el caballo. (I touch the cat, the dog, the sheep, and the horse.)
Pásame la falda verde o la falda azul, por favor. (Pass me the green skirt or the blue skirt, please.)
No me duelen ni los dedos, ni la mano, ni el brazo. (Neither my fingers, nor my hand, nor my arm hurts.)

Me gustan las manzanas pero no me gustan las piñas. (I like apples but I
don't like pineapples.)

rápidamente (rapidly); lentamente (slowly). These adverbs are used with
the verbs of motion. Children enjoy dramatizing in an exaggerated manner the
meaning of these two adverbs as they respond to the command or act out the
statement.
Camina rápidamente hacia la puerta, por favor. (Walk rapidly toward the
door, please.)
Camino lentamente hacia mi casa. (I walk slowly toward my house.)

muy (very); más (more); menos (less). These adverbs combine with the
preceding adverbs to describe how a movement should occur or is occurring.
Corre más rápidamente, Jorge. (Run more rapidly, George.)
Corre menos rápidamente. (Run less rapidly.)
Salto muy lentamente. (I am jumping very slowly.)

ahora (now); después (after, later, next). These adverbs help to order
events in time.
Ahora, pon los animales. Después, pon el árbol y la flor. (Now, put on the
animals. Next, put on the tree and the flower.)

hacia (toward). This preposition is used with the verbs camina, camino,
corre, corro, salta, and salto, as suggested in the description of these
verbs.

abierto, cerrado (open, closed); bonito, feo (pretty, ugly); nuevo, viejo
(new, old); limpio, sucio (clean, dirty); mucho, poco (a lot of--s., many--pl.;
little--s., few--pl.). It is helpful to teach adjective opposites together to
clarify their meanings. Whenever possible they should be introduced with objects that illustrate their meanings clearly. For example, a very dirty shoe
and a clean shoe can illustrate "dirty" and "clean." Later the adjectives can
be suggested by flash cards: an illustration of a pretty princess suggests
"pretty" and a witch suggests "ugly."
As with the color adjectives, the children need to imagine that when
these flash cards are placed next to an object, the object takes on the quali-
ty illustrated by the flash card. A flash card with many dots can indicate
"many" and when placed next to a toy sheep would indicate "many sheep."
As before, using the adjective first with masculine nouns, then with fem--
inine nouns, and last with plural nouns, will clarify noun-adjective agreement
for children. The children will enjoy discovering the many ways these adjectives can be used with the nouns they have learned.
Dibuja un ojo cerrado y un ojo abierto. (Draw one eye closed and one eye
open.)
Veo una blusa bonita. (I see a pretty blouse.)
No me gusta la falda vieja pero me gusta la falda nueva. (I don't like the
old skirt but I like the new skirt.)
Tengo las manos muy sucias. (I have very dirty hands.)
Como mucho cereal. (I eat a lot of cereal.)

(tengo) calor (I'm hot); (tengo) frío (I'm cold); (tengo) hambre (I'm
hungry); (tengo) sed (I'm thirsty); (tengo) sueño (I'm sleepy). These expressions add to the descriptions that children can make about themselves and lend
themselves well to the dramatization of feelings.

la amiga, el amigo (friend--f., m.)
Soy el amigo de Juan. (I am John's friend.)

el cumpleaños (birthday). Since children enjoy birthdays so much this is
a good area in which to expand the vocabulary if time permits. Other words
that might be added are la torta (cake), el regalo (present), el globo (bal-
loon), la vela (candle), and la fiesta (party). They can describe what they
see in illustrations or in photographs from their own birthday parties. For
example:
  Hay una torta bonita en el aula. (There is a pretty cake in the classroom.)
  Veo ocho velas en la torta. (I see eight candles on the cake.)
  Me gustan las fiestas de cumpleaños. (I like birthday parties.)

la granja (farm). This word can be used with the names of farm animals
and tractor (tractor) that are taught in this level. Children can describe
what they see in illustrations of farms.
  Veo la granja. (I see the farm.)
  Hay muchos animales en la granja. (There are many animals on the farm.)
  Veo dos tractores en la granja. (I see two tractors on the farm.)

Vocabulario Básico (Basic Vocabulary)

The discussion of the new nouns of the basic vocabulary areas focuses on
their usage with the new verbs and modifiers in this level, even though in the
classroom the material of the previous level is reviewed and used with this
new material. The discussion of each of the following levels continues this
pattern.
     Since teachers have a good understanding of the use of the teaching ma-
terials in the class activities, they are not listed again. Numbers and color
words continue to be used as in Level 1.
     Note that the adjectives are used as modifiers of nouns in this level;
for example, el cerdo limpio (the clean pig). When the "to be" verbs, ser and
estar, are introduced in the next level, the adjectives will also be used as
predicate adjectives; for example: El cerdo está limpio. (The pig is clean.)

Los alimentos (Foods)

Nouns	Verbs		Modifiers	
el agua	bebo	paso	los números	sucio
el azúcar	como	pongo	nuevo	mucho
el cereal	dibuja	saco	viejo	poco
el desayuno	dibujo	tengo	limpio	
el jugo	me gusta	toco		
la leche	me gustan	veo		
el pan	hay			
la tostada				

Examples of sentences
Dibuja dos tostadas, por favor. (Draw two pieces of toast, please.)
Tengo mucha sed. Pásame el jugo de manzana, por favor. (I am very thirsty.
  Pass me the apple juice, please.)
Me gusta el desayuno. Como el cereal y bebo mucha leche. (I like break-
  fast. I eat cereal and drink a lot of milk.)

Los animales (Animals)

Nouns	Verbs		Modifiers	
el animal	dibuja	pongo	los colores	viejo
el caballo	dibujo	saco	los números	limpio
el cerdo	me gusta	tengo	bonito	sucio
la gallina	me gustan	tiro	feo	mucho
la oveja	hay	toco	nuevo	poco
la vaca	paso	veo		

Examples of sentences
Veo el caballo marrón. Pásame el caballo marrón, por favor. (I see the
  brown horse. Pass me the brown horse, please.)
¿Cuántos animales hay? Hay doce animales. (How many animals are there?
  There are twelve animals.)
Pongo la oveja y saco el cerdo. (I put on the sheep and I remove the pig.)

La casa (House)

Nouns	Verbs		Modifiers	
el garaje	abre	paso	los colores	nuevo
la puerta	abro	pongo	los números	viejo
la ventana	cierra	regreso	abierto	limpio
	cierro	saco	cerrado	sucio
	dibuja	tengo	bonito	mucho
	dibujo	toco	feo	poco
	me gusta	veo		
	me gustan	voy		
	hay			

Examples of sentences
Abro la puerta del garaje. (I open the garage door.)
Regreso a mi casa. (I am returning home.)
Dibujo muchas ventanas en la casa azul. (I draw many windows in the blue
  house.)

El cuerpo humano (Body parts)

Nouns	Verbs		Modifiers	
el brazo	dibuja	paso	los colores	limpio
la cara	dibujo	pongo	los números	sucio
el dedo	me duele	saco	bonito	mucho
la lengua	me duelen	tengo	feo	poco
la oreja	me gusta	tiro		
	me gustan	toco		
	hay	veo		

Examples of sentences
Pongo la lengua. (I put on the tongue.)
Me duelen los brazos. (My arms hurt.)
Dibujo una cara fea. Dibujo un ojo grande y tres orejas. (I draw an ugly
  face. I draw a large eye and three ears.)

La escuela (School)

Nouns	Verbs		Modifiers	
la alumna	ayudo	paso	los números	viejo
el alumno	camino	pongo	abierto	limpio
el aula	como	regreso	cerrado	sucio
la escuela	corro	saco	bonito	mucho
el profesor	dibuja	salto	feo	poco
la profesora	dibujo	tengo	nuevo	
	estoy	toco		
	me gusta	veo		
	me gustan	voy		
	hay			

Examples of sentences
Ayudo a mi profesora. (I help my teacher.)
No me gustan las aulas sucias. (I don't like dirty classrooms.)
Hay muchos alumnos en mi aula. Hay quince niñas y catorce niños. (There
  are many students in my classroom. There are fifteen girls and fourteen
  boys.)

La familia (Family)

Nouns	Verbs		Modifiers	
la abuela	amo	paso	los números	viejo
el abuelo	ayudo	pongo	bonito	mucho
los abuelos	dibuja	saco	feo	poco
	dibujo	tengo		
	me gusta	toco		
	me gustan	veo		
	hay			

Examples of sentences
Pongo la abuela y el abuelo. (I put on the grandmother and the grand-
  father.)
Amo a mis abuelos. (I love my grandparents.)
Tengo dos abuelos y una abuela. (I have two grandfathers and a grand-
  mother.)

La ropa (Clothing)

Nouns	Verbs		Modifiers	
la blusa	dibuja	pongo	los colores	viejo
la camisa	dibujo	saco	los números	limpio
la falda	me gusta	tengo	bonito	sucio
los pantalones	me gustan	tiro	feo	mucho
el zapato	hay	toco	nuevo	poco
	llevo puesto	veo		
	paso			

Examples of sentences
Paso la blusa nueva a María. (I pass the new blouse to Mary.)
Llevo puesta una camisa verde y blanca. (I am wearing a green and white
  shirt.)

Me gustan los zapatos negros pero no me gustan los zapatos azules. (I like the black shoes but I don't like the blue shoes.)

Transporte (Transportation)

Nouns	Verbs		Modifiers	
la bicicleta	dibuja	pongo	los colores	viejo
el tractor	dibujo	saco	los números	limpio
	me gusta	tengo	bonito	sucio
	me gustan	toco	feo	mucho
	hay	veo	nuevo	poco
	paso	voy		

Examples of sentences

No tengo una bicicleta nueva. (I don't have a new bicycle.)
Hay muchos tractores en Iowa. (There are many tractors in Iowa.)
Veo dos bicicletas marrones. (I see two brown bicycles.)

V O C A B U L A R Y

Los Verbos

abre*	corro	pongo
abro	dibuja*	regreso
amo	dibujo	saco
ayudo	duele	salta*
bebo	duelen	salto
camina*	gusta	soy
camino	gustan	tengo
cierra*	hay	tiro
cierro	voy+	toco
como	llevo puesto	veo
corre*	paso	

Vocabulario Básico

Los alimentos
el agua
el azúcar
el cereal
el desayuno
el jugo
la leche
el pan
la tostada

Los animales
el animal
el caballo
el cerdo
la gallina
la oveja
la vaca

La casa
el garaje
la puerta
la ventana

Los colores
azul
marrón
verde

El cuerpo humano
el brazo
la cara
el dedo
la lengua
la oreja

La escuela
la alumna
el alumno
el aula
la escuela
el profesor
la profesora

La familia
la abuela
el abuelo
los abuelos

Los números
11-20

---

*Command form of the verb.
+Verbs are listed according to the alphabetical order of the infinitives.

La ropa
la blusa
la camisa
la falda
los pantalones
el zapato

Transporte
la bicicleta
el tractor

Oraciones Interrogativas
¿Cuántos años tienes?
¿Cuántos ——— hay?
¿Qué ves?
¿Dónde te duele?

Expresiones Comunes
buenas noches
buenas tardes
hasta luego

Vocabulario Suplementario

yo	lentamente	limpio
mi, mis	muy	sucio
me	más	mucho
mí	menos	poco
un, una	ahora	(tengo) calor
unos, unas	después	(tengo) frío
a, al, a la	hacia	(tengo) hambre
sí	abierto	(tengo) sed
no	cerrado	(tengo) sueño
y	bonito	la amiga
o	feo	el amigo
ni	nuevo	el cumpleaños
pero	viejo	la granja
rápidamente		

The third person singular form of the verbs is introduced in this level. The awareness of word endings that children have developed in making noun-adjective agreement will help them hear the difference between the <u>o</u> ending of the first person singular and the <u>a</u> and <u>e</u> endings of the third person singular. This is the only difference between first and third persons of regularly conjugated verbs.

The commands are helpful in introducing the third person singular. Now, instead of children describing their own actions in response to a command, they as observers can report the actions of others; for example:

María: Juan, pásame la leche, por favor. (John, pass me the milk, please.)
Observer, as John passes the milk to Mary: Juan pasa la leche a María. (John passes the milk to Mary.)

The description of the action is first modeled by the teacher, then practiced by the children. When they have learned how to make several descriptions, the children take turns being observers. They especially enjoy being observers when they assume the roles of radio or television announcers who speak into microphones. Toy microphones can be provided for this purpose. In the following example, note that the observer describes the actions of the participants, not what they say.

Jorge: Gloria, pásame el té, la leche y el azúcar, por favor. (Gloria, pass me the tea, the milk, and the sugar, please.)
Observer, as Gloria passes the objects: Gloria pasa el té, la leche y el azúcar a Jorge. (Gloria passes the tea, the milk, and the sugar to George.)
Jorge: Gracias. (Thank you.)
Gloria: De nada. (You're welcome.)
Observer, as George puts the milk and sugar in the tea and drinks the tea: Jorge pone la leche y el azúcar en el té. Él bebe el té. (George puts the milk and the sugar in the tea. He drinks the tea.)

Another way to use the third person singular is for an observer to describe a child who is pantomiming a feeling. Later a short series of actions and feelings can be described:

Observer: María tiene hambre. (Mary is hungry.) No tiene ni un huevo, ni un plátano, ni una naranja. (She doesn't have an egg, a banana, or an orange.) Dibuja una naranja en la pizarra. (She draws an orange on the blackboard.) ¡Come la naranja! (She is eating the orange!) María está feliz

25

porque ahora no tiene hambre.   (Mary is happy because now she is not hungry.)

The third person singular is also helpful for children's self-descriptions. Using the new vocabulary of this level, the children are able to describe their family members, pets, and possessions.

Mi casa está cerca de la escuela.   (My house is close to the school.)
Es de color amarillo.   (It is yellow.)
Tiene dos dormitorios, un cuarto de baño, una cocina, un comedor y una sala. (It has two bedrooms, a bathroom, a kitchen, a dining room, and a living room.)
Hay quince ventanas y cinco puertas en mi casa.   (There are fifteen windows and five doors in my house.)
Me gusta mucho mi casa.   (I like my house very much.)

Having heard the self-descriptions made in Level 2, the children are well acquainted with their companions and can now learn to describe them. First the teacher can make the description and ask the children to determine which classmate is being described. When the children know who it is, they repeat the description to practice the new verb forms and vocabulary. When they are familiar with them, they begin describing their companions independently.

The third person singular of two verbs that are useful in description, ser (to be) and estar (to be), are introduced in this level. It is helpful to begin with ser, practicing the use of es (is) with the familiar color adjectives as predicate adjectives. For example: La falda es negra. (The skirt is black.) Since the children have learned to make noun-adjective agreement they do not have difficulty making the agreement necessary between the noun, falda, and the predicate adjective, negra. The adjectives of size, grande, mediano, and pequeño (large or big, medium, and small) are introduced with objects that clarify and contrast their meaning. Children practice the use of the adjectives of color and size extensively until they can form sentences using the predicate adjectives correctly.

Next, the third person singular of estar, está (is), is introduced and practiced with the adverbs of position: cerca de (close to) and lejos de (far away from). For example: El libro está cerca de Juan. (The book is close to John.) María está lejos de Gloria. (Mary is far away from Gloria.)

When both es (is) and está (is) are used easily in separate activities, children can begin to use them together in the same activity as in the description of illustrations or the scenes in the classroom.

Veo un bolígrafo y un libro.   (I see a pen and a book.)
El bolígrafo está cerca del libro.   (The pen is close to the book.)
El bolígrafo es rojo y negro.   (The pen is red and black.)
El libro es muy grande.   (The book is very large.)

In this level the remaining adjectives are used only with está (is) to avoid the change in meaning that occurs when ser (to be) and estar (to be) are interchanged. These adjectives are introduced gradually, contrasting opposites when possible: feliz, triste (happy, sad); caliente, frío (hot, cold); contento (content); enojado (angry); delicioso (delicious); and frito (fried). Children enjoy dramatizing the meaning of the adjectives of emotions while an observer describes what they are doing.

Remember that learning the correct usage of the verbs ser (to be) and estar (to be) is difficult even for advanced language students. The children

will make errors in the use of these two verbs when they are creating their
own sentences. Instead of relying on verbal explanations concerning the use
of each verb, they will learn correct usage more adequately by having sufficient time to become accustomed to hearing and using the verbs correctly. The
teacher must provide the children with activities so that they can practice
the use of these verbs. The teacher also needs to analyze the errors the
children are making in order to plan activities that will help correct their
misunderstandings.

These two verbs can be practiced with flash cards that represent the adjectives and adverbs of position. The flash cards are mixed and placed in a
pile face down. From this pile the children take turns drawing a card. The
words represented on the cards they choose must be used correctly in a sentence with either es (is) or está (is). If their sentences are correct, they
keep the cards; if not, the cards go to the bottom of the pile to reappear
later. A number of variations to this activity can be made. For example, if
an incorrect sentence is corrected by another, that person keeps the card instead of its being returned to the bottom of the pile.

The infinitives of regularly conjugated verbs of the first conjugation
(ar) and the second conjugation (er) are taught in this level. It is helpful
to teach the infinitives after children learn the third person singular form
well, since the infinitives of these verbs are made by adding the r sound to
the ending of the third person singular, i.e., está, estar; corre, correr.
The infinitives are used with other verbs, as in the examples that follow.
The final example shows an infinitive used with the verb ir (to go) to express
a future idea while using the present tense.

Él ayuda a tirar la pelota grande. (He helps to throw the big ball.)
A Gloria le gusta dibujar. (Gloria likes to draw.)
Juan no puede comer ahora. (John can't eat now.)
Ella quiere tener la gallina. (She wants to have the hen.)
María no va a ir a la casa de sus abuelos. (Mary is not going to go to her
grandparents' house.)

The teacher introduces the infinitives by gradually including them in
sentences. As the children discover the infinitives and begin to use them in
sentences, the teacher will need to caution them that not all verb infinitives
are formed in the same way. The infinitives of the irregularly conjugated
verbs and verbs of the third conjugation (ir) that are not formed in this way
are included in Level 4.

SELECTION   AND   USE   OF   VOCABULARY

Los Verbos (Verbs)
Several new verbs are added in this level besides ser and estar. The
verb forms in which the new verbs are introduced and examples of their usage
are included here. The first three verbs are used with infinitives.

puedo, puede (to be able [to], can)
Él puede dibujar muy bien. (He can draw very well.)
María no puede correr rápidamente. (Mary can't run rapidly.)

quiero, quiere (to want)
Gloria quiere comer ahora. (Gloria wants to eat now.)

Ella no quiere llevar puesto el vestido anaranjado. (She doesn't want to wear the orange dress.)

tengo que, tiene que (to have to). This verb is taught as a way of expressing strong personal necessity.
Jorge tiene que regresar a la escuela. (George has to return to school.)
Él tiene que beber el jugo de naranja. (He has to drink the orange juice.)

viajo, viaja, viajar (to travel). This verb is used with words of la naturaleza (nature) to express where one is traveling. The teacher can also introduce the Spanish names of cities, states, or countries the children would like to visit. The verb forms of ir (to go) combine with this infinitive to express a future idea. The day of the week when this action will take place can be stated with the words from el calendario (calendar).
A mi mamá le gusta viajar a las montañas. (My mom likes to travel to the mountains.)
Mi hermano va a viajar el viernes. (My brother is going to travel Friday.)

Oraciones Interrogativas (Interrogative Sentences)
Three interrogative sentences are introduced. The first sentence employs the interrogative adónde (where) that is used with verbs of motion. It is: ¿Adónde (va Juan)? (Where [is John going]?) The answer to this question uses a phrase, for example, a la escuela (to the school): Juan va a la escuela. (John is going to the school.) Any of the words introduced in the two vocabulary areas la casa (house) or la naturaleza (nature) can be substituted for la escuela (school).
The second question is: ¿De qué color (es la blusa)? (What color [is the blouse]?) The answer to this question uses a predicate adjective: La blusa (es amarilla). (The blouse [is yellow].)
¿Por qué (estás triste)? (Why [are you sad]?) is the third question. It is used with the expression of feelings and emotions in this level; in the next level it is used more extensively in dialogue and conversation. The word porque (because) is also taught in this level for use in the answer; for example: Estoy triste porque mi papá tiene que viajar mañana a Madrid. (I am sad because my dad has to travel tomorrow to Madrid.)

Expresiones Comunes (Common Expressions)
Included here is a question and several answers that are used traditionally in greeting another person. The question employs the intimate form of you, tú (as used in the commands), since it is used with children. In the next level, in which the intimate and formal forms of "you" are contrasted, the same question uses the formal form of "you." The question is: ¿Cómo estás? (How are you?) Three answers are included. The first two answers are followed by the question ¿Y tú? (And you?), as indicated: Estoy muy bien, gracias. ¿Y tú? (I am very well, thank you. And you?) Estoy regular, gracias. ¿Y tú? (I am not bad, thank you. And you?) The last answer is: Estoy muy mal. (I am very sick.) Since this answer requires a sympathetic comment from the inquirer, one is included: ¡Qué lástima! (What a pity!)
The three answers can be suggested by differing facial expressions drawn on flash cards. The children practice using the three different answers by choosing flash cards while their eyes are closed and answering the questions according to the expression on the cards that they chose.

Vocabulario Suplementario (Supplementary Vocabulary)
él, ella (he, she--subject; him, her--object of preposition). The sub-

ject pronouns of the third person singular are not used except for emphasis or clarification.

¡Él lleva puestas botas sucias, yo no! (He wears dirty boots, I don't!)
Ella es mi hermana. (She is my sister.)
María pasa la naranja a ella. (Mary passes the orange to her.)
A él le gusta el café frío. (He likes cold coffee.)

su, sus (his, her)
Su casa es muy grande. (His/her house is very large.)
Sus ojos son azules. (His/her eyes are blue.)

le (to him, to her). This pronoun is used as an indirect object with the verbs gustar (to please) and doler (to hurt).
A Gloria le gustan los panqueques. (Gloria likes pancakes.)
A él le duele el pie. (His foot hurts.)

nadie (nobody)
No hay nadie en la sala. (There isn't anyone in the living room.)

de, del, de la (of, from, to)
La hermana de Juan es muy bonita. (John's sister is very pretty.)
El vestido nuevo es de mi abuela. (The new dress is from my grandmother.)
El lago está cerca del bosque. (The lake is close to the woods.)
Mi casa está lejos de la casa de Jorge. (My house is far away from George's house.)

este, esta (this--m., f.); aquel, aquella (that--m., f.). The limiting adjectives are taught only in the singular at this time. They are taught in the plural when the plural forms of the verbs are taught in Level 5. It is helpful to teach "this" and "that" at the same time to clarify their meanings.
Este lápiz es de Gloria y aquel lápiz es de Juan. (This pencil is Gloria's and that pencil is John's.)
Esta bota es de María y aquella bota es de Gloria. (This boot is Mary's and that boot is Gloria's.)

aquí (here); allí (there). It is helpful to teach "here" and "there" at the same time to clarify their meanings.
Pon el libro aquí y pon el papel allí. (Put the book here and put the paper there.)
Jorge, corre hacia aquí y Juan, salta hacia allí. (George, run toward here, and John, jump toward there.)

con (with)
Él viaja con sus padres. (He is traveling with his parents.)
Jorge dibuja con la tiza. (George draws with the chalk.)

conmigo (with me)
Ella regresa a la escuela conmigo. (She returns to school with me.)

también (also, too); tampoco (neither, not either). Children first use these expressions in descriptions as they compare themselves or another child to the one being described.

Él tiene nueve años también. (He is nine years old also.)
María no tiene hermanos tampoco. (Mary doesn't have brothers either.)

    todo (all, every); nada (nothing, not anything). Using a large group of
objects of one kind, i.e., animals, numbers, clothing, the children take turns
dividing the objects among themselves and state what each child has or doesn't
have.
Gloria tiene todos los animales. (Gloria has all the animals.)
Juan no tiene nada. (John doesn't have anything.)
Él no tiene nada tampoco. (He doesn't have anything either.)

    porque (because)
Jorge está feliz porque tiene un perro nuevo. (George is happy because he
has a new dog.)
    (el sábado) que viene (next Saturday)
Ella va a viajar a California el sábado que viene. (She is going to travel
to California next Saturday.)
Mi papá va a ir a España la semana que viene. (My dad is going to go to
Spain next week.

    cerca de (close to); lejos de (far from)
Mi pupitre está lejos de la pizarra. (My desk is far from the blackboard.)
Mi casa está cerca de su casa. (My house is close to his/her house.)

    feliz, triste (happy, sad); caliente, frío (hot, cold); contento (con-
tent); enojado (angry); delicioso (delicious); frito (fried). These adjec-
tive opposites are introduced together and contrasted.
Juan está triste porque Pedro está enojado. (John is sad because Peter is
angry.)
María pasa el café caliente a Gloria. (Mary passes the hot coffee to
Gloria.)
No estoy enojado, estoy contento ahora. (I'm not angry, I'm content now.)
Los huevos fritos son deliciosos. (Fried eggs are delicious.)

    grande (large, big); mediano (medium); pequeño (small). It is helpful to
first teach the extremes (large and small) so that the contrast in size is
more noticeable.
María tiene el pato grande, Juan tiene el pato pequeño y yo tengo el pato
mediano. (Mary has the large duck, John has the small duck, and I have the
medium duck.)

    el dibujo (drawing)
Jorge ayuda a Juan con su dibujo. (George helps John with his drawing.)

    el viaje (trip)
Gloria está de viaje a París. (Gloria is on a trip to Paris.)

Vocabulario Básico (Basic Vocabulary)
    The description of the usage of the basic vocabulary is organized in the
same manner as that of the previous level.

Los alimentos (Foods)
    The vocabulary included in this level with the vocabulary in previous

levels represents a common breakfast in the United States. Additional words can be added if the interest and ability of the children permit, for example, syrup, butter. If the class meets closer to lunchtime than to breakfast, this vocabulary can be exchanged with the vocabulary common to lunches taught in the next level so that children first learn the vocabulary in which they have most interest at the time of day when the class meets.

Nouns	Verbs			Modifiers
el café	bebe	pasa	saca	los colores
el chocolate	beber	pasar	sacar	los números
el huevo	come	pone	es*	caliente
la naranja	comer	poner	tiene	frío
el panqueque	dibuja	puedo	tengo que	delicioso
el té	dibujar	puede	tiene que	frito
el tocino	está	quiero	toco	grande
	estar	quiere	tocar	mediano
		ve		pequeño

Examples of sentences
Ella tiene dos panqueques pequeños. (She has two small pancakes.)
A mi papá le gusta el café muy caliente. (My dad likes very hot coffee.)
Juan no quiere comer los huevos fritos. (John doesn't want to eat fried eggs.)

Los animales (Animals)

Nouns	Verbs			Modifiers
el pato	ayuda	estar	salta	los colores
el pez	ayudar	va*	saltar	los números
la rana	bebe	se llama	saca	feliz
la tortuga	beber	pasa	sacar	triste
	camina	pasar	es	contento
	caminar	puedo	tiene	enojado
	cierra	puede	tengo que	grande
	come	pone	tiene que	mediano
	comer	poner	tira	pequeño
	corre	quiero	tirar	
	dibuja	quiere	toca	
	dibujar	regresa	tocar	
	está	regresar	ve	
			vive	

Examples of sentences
Su rana salta muy rápidamente. (His/her frog jumps very rapidly.)
El pato de Gloria se llama Pedro. (The name of Gloria's duck is Peter.)
La tortuga grande vive en el mar. (The big turtle lives in the sea.)

El calendario (Calendar)
    The verb va is used with an infinitive for the expression of a future idea.

---

    *Verbs are listed according to the alphabetical order of the infinitives.

Nouns		Verbs	Modifiers
el día	miércoles	es	los números
hoy	jueves	hay	feliz
mañana	viernes	va	triste
la semana	sábado		
lunes	domingo		
martes			

Examples of sentences

Hoy es lunes. (Today is Monday.)

Hay siete días en una semana. (There are seven days in a week.)

Hoy es un día muy feliz. (Today is a very happy day.)

Mañana Juan va a caminar a la escuela. (Tomorrow John is going to walk to school.)

La casa (House)

Nouns	Verbs			Modifiers
la cocina	abre	dibujar	regresa	los colores
el comedor	camina	estoy	regresar	los números
el cuarto	caminar	está	salta	frío
el cuarto de baño	cierra	estar	saltar	grande
el dormitorio	come	va	es	mediano
la sala	comer	puedo	tengo que	pequeño
	corre	puede	tiene que	
	correr	quiero	toca	
	dibuja	quiere	tocar	
			ve	

Examples of sentences

Él abre la puerta del comedor. (He opens the dining room door.)

Jorge no puede correr ni en la cocina ni en la sala. (George can't run in the kitchen nor in the living room.)

El cuarto de baño es muy pequeño pero la sala es grande. (The bathroom is very small but the living room is large.)

El cuerpo humano (Body parts)

Nouns	Verbs			Modifiers
el cuello	dibuja	puede	tiene	los colores
el cuerpo	dibujar	pone	tengo que	los números
el pie	está	poner	tiene que	grande
la pierna	estar	quiero	tira	mediano
	pasa	quiere	tirar	pequeño
	pasar	saca	toca	
	puedo	sacar	tocar	
		es	ve	

Examples of sentences

Este pie es muy grande. (This foot is very large.)

A mi hermano le duele todo el cuerpo. (All of my brother's body hurts.)

Ella dibuja el pie con la tiza. (She draws the foot with the chalk.)

La escuela (School)

Nouns	Verbs			Modifiers
el bolígrafo	abre	pasa	saltar	los colores
el borrador	camina	pasar	saca	los números
el lápiz	caminar	puedo	sacar	grande
el libro	cierra	puede	es	mediano
el papel	corre	pone	tiene	pequeño
la pizarra	correr	poner	tengo que	
el pupitre	dibuja	quiero	tiene que	
la tiza	dibujar	quiere	tira	
	está	regresa	tirar	
	estar	regresar	toca	
	va	salta	tocar	
			ve	

Examples of sentences

María corre hacia su pupitre. (Mary runs toward her desk.)

Ella dibuja en el papel con el bolígrafo. (She draws on the paper with the pen.)

El profesor va a la pizarra y dibuja un pato. (The teacher goes to the blackboard and draws a duck.

La familia (Family)

Nouns	Verbs	Modifiers
el bebé	All verbs and verb forms can	los números
la familia	be used with this vocabulary.	feliz
la hermana		triste
el hermano		contento
los hermanos		enojado
la madre		grande
el padre		mediano
los padres		pequeño

Examples of sentences

Juan tiene tres hermanas y un hermano. (John has three sisters and one brother.

La familia de Jorge es grande pero la familia de Gloria es pequeña. (George's family is large but Gloria's family is small.)

Él tiene que viajar mañana con sus padres. (He has to travel tomorrow with his parents.)

La naturaleza (Nature)

Nouns	Verbs			Modifiers
el bosque	camina	pasa	sacar	los colores
el lago	caminar	pasar	es	los números
el mar	corre	puedo	tiene	grande
la montaña	correr	puede	tengo que	mediano
el valle	dibuja	pone	tiene que	pequeño
	dibujar	poner	toca	
	estoy	quiero	tocar	

está	quiere	ve
estar	regresa	viajo
va	regresar	viaja
se llama	saca	viajar
		vive

Examples of sentences

Jorge pasa la montaña pequeña a ella. (George passes the small mountain to her.)

Él no ve los peces en el lago. (He doesn't see the fish in the water.)

A ella le gusta viajar al mar con sus abuelos. (She likes to travel to the sea with her grandparents.)

La ropa (Clothing)

Nouns	Verbs			Modifiers
la bota	dibuja	puede	tiene	los colores
el calcetín	dibujar	pone	tengo que	los números
el pijama	está	poner	tiene que	grande
la ropa	estar	quiero	tira	mediano
el suéter	llevo puesto	quiere	tirar	pequeño
el vestido	llevar puesto	saca	toca	
	pasa	sacar	tocar	
	pasar	es	ve	
	puedo			

Examples of sentences

El bebé lleva puesto pijama. (The baby is wearing pajamas.)

Él tiene dos suéteres nuevos. (He has two new sweaters.)

María lleva puesto un vestido morado y blanco. (Mary is wearing a purple and white dress.)

El transporte (Transportation)

Nouns	Verbs			Modifiers
el barco	corre	puedo	tiene	los colores
el bote	correr	puede	tengo que	los números
	dibuja	pone	tiene que	grande
	dibujar	poner	toca	mediano
	estoy	quiero	tocar	pequeño
	está	quiere	ve	
	estar	regresa	viajo	
	va	regresar	viaja	
	se llama	saca	viajar	
	pasa	sacar	vive	
	pasar	es		

Examples of sentences

Mi hermano tiene un bote pequeño. (My brother has a small boat.)

Mi abuelo regresa en barco el domingo que viene. (My grandfather returns by ship next Sunday.)

Su padre va a viajar en barco. (His/her father is going to travel by ship.)

V O C A B U L A R Y

Los Verbos

abre	está	saca
ama	estar	sacar
ayuda	va*	salta
ayudar	se llama	saltar
bebe	lleva puesto	es*
beber	llevar puesto	tiene
camina	pasa	tengo que
caminar	pasar	tiene que
cierra	puedo	tira
come	puede	tirar
comer	pone	toca
corre	poner	tocar
correr	quiero	ve
dibuja	quiere	viajo
dibujar	regresa	viaja
estoy	regresar	viajar
		vive

Vocabulario Básico

Los alimentos
el café
el chocolate
el huevo
la naranja
el panqueque
el té
el tocino

Los animales
el pato
el pez
la rana
la tortuga

El calendario
el día
hoy
mañana
la semana
lunes
martes
miércoles
jueves
viernes
sábado
domingo

La casa
la cocina
el comedor
el cuarto
el cuarto de baño
el dormitorio
la sala

Los colores
amarillo
anaranjado
morado

El cuerpo humano
el cuello
el cuerpo
el pie
la pierna

La escuela
el bolígrafo
el borrador
el lápiz
el libro
el papel
la pizarra
el pupitre
la tiza

La familia
el bebé
la familia
la hermana
el hermano
los hermanos
la madre
el padre
los padres

La naturaleza
el bosque
el lago
el mar
la montaña
el valle

Los números
21-50

La ropa
la bota
el calcetín
el pijama
la ropa
el suéter
el vestido

Transporte
el barco
el bote

---

*Verbs are listed according to the alphabetical order of the infinitives.

Oraciones Interrogativas
¿Adónde (va Juan)?
¿De qué color (es la blusa)?
¿Por qué (estás triste)?

Expresiones Comunes
¿Cómo estás?
Estoy muy bien, gracias.
Estoy regular, gracias.
¿Y tú?
Estoy muy mal.
¡Qué lástima!

Vocabulario Suplementario

él, ella	tampoco	frío
su, sus	todo	contento
le	nada	enojado
nadie	porque	delicioso
de, del, de la	(el sábado) que viene	frito
este, esta	cerca de	grande
aquel, aquella	lejos de	mediano
aquí	feliz	pequeño
allí	triste	el dibujo
con	caliente	el viaje
conmigo		
también		

LEVEL 4

The introduction of the second person singular makes it possible for the children to address other persons directly and engage in conversation--the informal, spontaneous exchange of thoughts and feelings. Since this use of the language is new to them, the children are restricted at first to asking and answering the questions taught in earlier levels. To help them gain experience in conversing, the development of dialogues is emphasized. Dialogues are conversations planned by the children and their teacher around specific situations or themes. The verbal exchange of the final dialogue is practiced by the children until it flows easily, simulating natural conversation. Dialogues give the children experience in the use of the language that is later helpful to them in conversing.

Both forms of the second person singular, the intimate tú (you) and the formal usted (you), are introduced. Extensive practice with these two Spanish forms is needed to clarify their usage. The first second person form taught is the intimate tú (you). Children are already somewhat familiar with this form since it is used in all the questions in the first two levels and in one of the questions of the third level. Reviewing these questions is a good place to start in teaching the intimate. The questions are:

¿Cómo te llamas? (What is your name?)
¿Dónde vives? (Where do you live?)
¿Cuántos años tienes? (How old are you?)
¿Qué ves? (What do you see?)
¿Dónde te duele? (Where do you hurt?)
¿Por qué (estás triste)? (Why [are you sad]?)

The other questions taught in Level 3 can be changed to the second person intimate:

¿Adónde (vas)? (Where [are you going]?)
¿De qué color (es tu vestido)? (What color [is your dress]?)

The two new questions of this level, which are in the second person intimate, are introduced and practiced:

¿Cuál es tu dirección? (What is your address?)
¿Cuándo te vas de vacaciones? (When do you go away on vacation?)

Additional questions can be modeled by the teacher, using the interroga-

tives of these familiar questions with other vocabulary. Children can combine the questions and the answers they learn to make in the second person intimate into short conversations. Further practice of the intimate may involve
dialogues with children, family members, and good friends as the characters.

When children can use the intimate form easily, the formal usted (you) of
the second person singular is taught. The verb form used with usted is the
same as the verb form of the third person singular. In learning the use of
the formal usted the children are learning a new way to use an already familiar verb form. Children can practice the use of the formal in the same way as
they did the intimate--by asking questions using that verb form. Short conversations are made and dialogues are developed--for example, dialogues between two adults who have just met, between shop clerk and adult customer, or
between doctor and adult patient.

The intimate and the formal are used together only after they have been
practiced extensively in separate dialogues. They can be used together in
dialogues in which the characters are, for example, a police officer and child
or shop clerk and child.

With the introduction of conversation and dialogue in this level, a
change is made in the description of the basic vocabulary areas. In the first
three levels, examples of sentences are included to illustrate how the nouns,
verbs, and modifiers can be combined into sentences. In this level, in order
to utilize the vocabulary, examples of themes are included around which conversations and dialogues can be developed. Some of the themes suggested require only the intimate form of the second person singular, some require only
the formal form, and some require both the intimate and formal. The teacher
will choose the theme to correspond to the form of the second person singular
the children are practicing or the teacher can adapt the themes to that verb
form.

The dialogues and conversations can be acted out by the children themselves or with dolls or puppets. Specific articles of clothing or props will
help identify the roles. For example, a stethoscope can identify the doctor,
a pull toy can identify the child, and a purse can identify the mother.

The theme ideas plus others that the teacher might add are suggested to
the children. It is a good idea to ask for further suggestions from the children for they are very imaginative and will have good ideas of their own to
offer. Whenever possible the children's suggestions should be used. They appreciate having their ideas respected by adults and work even harder on ideas
that originate with them.

The teacher will make the final choice of theme, considering the feasi-
bility of its development with the vocabulary the children have learned and
the level of language ability they have attained. The teacher will decide
whether the children might be able to develop a spontaneous conversation
around it or whether a dialogue will need to be developed. If a dialogue is
chosen, developed, and learned, simple variations can be made in the theme and
the children can then create conversations around the variations.

For example, a theme suggested in the vocabulary area entitled la ropa
(clothing) is: A parent insists that a child wear warm winter clothing on a
cold day and the child resists. Variations of this theme that might be used
for conversation after the children have developed and learned the dialogue
are: A parent insists that a child wear cool summer clothing on a hot day and
the child resists, wanting to wear winter clothing. A parent insists that a
child wear the new shoes and the child resists, wanting to wear the old ones.
A parent insists that a child wear a clean pair of pants and the child resists, wanting to wear the dirty pair.

It is important that children help in developing dialogues to gain experience for creating dialogues and conversations on their own. The children
can brainstorm what might be said. When an incorrect statement is suggested,
the teacher asks the group to consider why it is incorrect and asks for a better one. The teacher records in writing or on tape the children's ideas and
with these ideas creates a dialogue outside of class time. The first dialogues need to be short but gradually the length can be increased.

The final dialogue that the teacher creates should have a realistic and
natural flow of conversation as used by native speakers. To attain this, the
teacher will need to include in the dialogue, along with the ideas that the
children have suggested, expressions that are new to the children. The children can learn these new expressions as they practice the dialogues. They are
encouraged to use them later in the conversations they create around the dialogue variations. As they learn these new expressions their use of the language will expand and become more like that of a native speaker.

It is wise not to overwhelm the children with too many new expressions;
to keep the dialogues in the present tense; and to employ the first, second,
and third person singular of the indicative as the most common verb forms.

Especially with the intimate form of the second person, a need for the
imperative will arise. Children already have been introduced to the imperative of the second person intimate with the commands in Level 1. Further
positive and negative commands needed in the dialogues are taught, but the imperative is not studied extensively at this time to avoid requiring children
to learn an additional verb form. They should be encouraged to use the new
commands by following what they learn in the dialogues. For example:

Madre: ¡Juan, come el huevo! (John, eat the egg!)
Padre: ¡María, no corras en la sala! (Mary, don't run in the living room!)

Besides learning to use the interrogatives discussed earlier in this section, it is important for children to learn other ways of asking questions
that are commonly used in native speech. Children can learn to change the
familiar declarative sentence pattern of subject-verb-complement to verb-
subject-complement to make a question with the second person form of the verbs
without the use of an interrogative. The subject pronoun of the second person intimate is not commonly expressed except for emphasis.

¿Quieres (tú) jugar en la nieve? (Do you want to play in the snow?)
¿Lavas (tú) los platos? (Do you wash the dishes?)
¿Es usted el médico? (Are you the doctor?)
¿Vive usted en Miami? (Do you live in Miami?)

Questions can be made by voice inflection, such as in the following
statement:

¿Tú quieres jugar en la nieve? (You want to play in the snow?)

Introducing children to making questions by voice inflection illustrates
and emphasizes the importance of developing expressive speech. In conversation, the voice as well as the whole body participates in communication. The
voice can be questioning, shocked, frightened, or sad or can express any other
emotion. The body adds to the meaning of the message that is transmitted in,
for example, the expression of the face, the movement and position of the
hands and arms, and the general tension of the body. Children can observe the

importance of these subtle actions as they communicate with their friends and family in English. They need to practice, perhaps by overexaggerating at first, the ways their own bodies and voices can help communicate the thoughts they express verbally in the second language. Expressive speech has to be emphasized when a second language is learned outside its cultural context, for the language seems artificial if it does not carry the same expressiveness that it does when used in actual situations.

The teacher introduces the completed dialogue to the children by expressive reading or dramatization. The children should be encouraged to try to understand from the context the meaning of new words that are introduced. Making intelligent guesses about the meaning of new words is a skill important to conversational ability that should be developed by the children.

The teacher will then determine who will play the various roles. Since the children need to practice the language, every child should have a role to learn. Several children can learn a role at the same time and take turns playing it, or, to reduce the number of children learning the same role at one time, the group can be divided and several dialogues developed at once. The small groups could then exchange dialogues so that each small group can learn each of the dialogues.

Since children do not see a written copy of the dialogue, a tape recorder can help the children learn their parts. The teacher can make a recording of the dialogue; one part of the group can use it while the teacher works with the other part of the group. This tape can be left in the school library or copies can be made so that the children can take them home to have further practice with their parts.

When a dialogue has been mastered by the children, a tape recording can be made while they present it. This tape, with the children's own voices, can be placed in a permanent and growing collection of completed dialogues and can be used for review. Children enjoy keeping copies of these completed dialogues themselves for it helps them appreciate the work they have done and the language they have learned.

When interest in a theme is high the dialogue is developed more extensively, numerous props are added, and a skit is created. Children often create skits on their own while at play and find this activity especially satisfying. They have excellent ideas for props and are eager to bring things from home to use as props. It is a good idea for the teacher to check with the parents first to ensure their cooperation.

When a skit has been polished it can be presented to parents and families, to students of the language in other classes, or to community groups. It is very rewarding for the children to have this opportunity to share what they have helped to create and to demonstrate their growing ability in the use of the language.

S E L E C T I O N   A N D   U S E   O F   V O C A B U L A R Y

Los Verbos (Verbs)

The infinitives of irregular verbs and the infinitives of the third conjugation (verbs that end in ir) are taught in this level. These verbs form their infinitives with changes other than the addition of r to the third person singular. For example, cierra changes to cerrar (to close) and va changes to ir (to go)(irregular verbs); and abre changes to abrir (to open) and vive changes to vivir (third conjugation verbs).

The children can learn the use of these infinitives through modeling.

The teacher needs to plan activities that require extensive use of these verbs so that the children can learn their formation and distinguish them from the verbs of the first and second conjugation. The fact that children have already been using the first and second conjugation verbs in the infinitive will help in making this distinction. These infinitives are found in the vocabulary at the end of the discussion of this level.

Other verbs introduced in this level are examined. The first two have been used in previous levels but are now used in new ways. Each verb given in the second person intimate is also taught in the second person formal.

llevo, llevas, lleva, llevar (to carry, take). This verb used without puesto can refer to any object that can be carried or taken away.
  ¿Llevas el automóvil al parque? (Are you taking the car to the park?)
  Llevo a mi hermano a visitar el jardín zoológico. (I take my brother to visit the zoo.)

me voy, te vas, se va, irse (to go away)
  ¿Cuándo te vas de vacaciones? (When are you going away on vacation?)
  Me voy el verano que viene. (I am going next summer.)

entiendo, entiendes, entiende, entender (to understand, comprehend); estudio, estudias, estudia, estudiar (to study); hablo, hablas, habla, hablar (to speak, talk). These three verbs can be used in a variety of ways; here they are all used to refer to languages, specifically to (el) inglés (English) and (el) español (Spanish) that are taught in this level.
  ¿Hablas español? (Do you speak Spanish?)
  Estudio español en la escuela. (I study Spanish in school.)
  Entiendo inglés pero no entiendo español. (I understand English but I don't understand Spanish.)

escucho, escuchas, escucha, escuchar (to listen to, to hear)
  ¿No escuchas el timbre? (Aren't you listening to the bell?)
  Me gusta escuchar los automóviles en la calle. (I like to hear the cars in the street.)

hace (calor, fresco, frío) (it's hot, cool, cold). Hace is used to refer to the weather when combined with words from the vocabulary area el clima (climate), as illustrated.
  Hace mucho calor en el verano. (It is very hot in the summer.)
  Hace fresco hoy. (It is cool today.)

juego, juegas, juega, jugar (to play). Who one is playing with can be stated with con (with). What one is playing in can be stated with en (in) and the words el barro (mud), la nieve (snow), la lluvia (rain), and el agua (water). The names of toys that children play with can also be taught and used with con (with).
  ¿Juegas en la nieve con Juan? (Do you play in the snow with John?)
  Tu madre está enojada porque juegas en el barro. (Your mother is angry because you are playing in the mud.)
  A ella le gusta jugar con una pelota. (She likes to play with a ball.)

lavo, lavas, lava, lavar (to wash)
  ¿Ayudas a tu papá a lavar el automóvil? (Do you help your father wash the car?)

Lavo mi bicicleta cuando está muy sucia.   (I wash my bicycle when it is very dirty.)

llueve, llover (to rain); nieva, nevar (to snow)
Puede nevar cuando hace mucho frío.   (It can snow when it is very cold.)
Llueve mucho en la primavera.   (It rains a lot in the spring.)

preparo, preparas, prepara, preparar (to prepare)
Preparo la gelatina para el almuerzo.   (I prepare the gelatin for lunch.)
¿Preparas el automóvil para el viaje?   (Are you preparing the car for the trip?)
Gloria prepara la casa para las visitas.   (Gloria is preparing the house for the visitors.)

me siento, te sientes, se siente (to feel)
Me siento peor.   Tengo que ir al médico ya.   (I feel worse.   I have to go to the doctor now.)
Juan se siente muy bien ahora.   (John feels very well now.)

vengo, vienes, viene, venir (to come)
¿Cuándo vienes a mi casa?   (When are you coming to my house?)
Mi abuela va a venir mañana.   (My grandmother is going to come tomorrow.)

visito, visitas, visita, visitar (to visit)
¿Visitas el jardín zoológico en el verano?   (Do you visit the zoo in the summer?)
Jorge visita a su abuelo en el invierno.   (George visits his grandfather in the winter.)

Oraciones Interrogativas (Interrogative Sentences)

Two new interrogatives are taught in this level. Cuál (which, what) can be used to ask one's address: ¿Cuál es (tu dirección)? (What is [your address]?) To answer this question with their street name and number, children will need to learn some numbers above 100. This will introduce them to the higher numbers that are taught in Level 5. For example: Mi dirección es calle Lincoln, número 1023. (My address is 1023 Lincoln Street.) The interrogative cuál (which) can also be used to ask which of several objects belongs to someone. For example: ¿Cuál es tu chaqueta? (Which is your jacket?)

The other interrogative taught is cuándo (when). It is suggested for use in the question: ¿Cuándo (te vas de vacaciones)? (When [do you go away on vacation]?) It can be used in asking when any activity takes place. In this level the answers employ days of the week or seasons; the next level uses months of the year also in the answers. The expression of a future idea in the answer to questions using this interrogative are possible with the verb ir (to go) and an infinitive; for example: Voy a irme de vacaciones en el verano. (I am going to go away on vacation in the summer.)

Expresiones Comunes (Common Expressions)

A question taught in the second person intimate in the previous level is now taught in the formal: ¿Cómo está usted? (How are you?) With the introduction of the first person singular of the verb sentirse (to feel), another way to answer this question is taught: Me siento (mejor). (I feel [better].) This expression can also be used with the second and third person singular to describe others: Veo que te sientes mejor. (I see that you feel better.)

Juan se siente mejor hoy. (John feels better today.) With the introduction of _peor_ (worse) a contrasting idea can be expressed with this verb: Me siento peor. (I feel worse.)

Because of the extensive use of the second person singular in this level, an informal greeting used with close friends is taught: ¡Hola! ¿Qué tal? (Hi! How are you?)

The extensive use of dialogue and conversation makes the learning of more exclamatory statements useful. Several are suggested: ¡Qué lluvia tan fuerte! (What a heavy rain!) ¡Qué animal feroz! (What a ferocious animal!) Others can be added as needed.

Vocabulario Suplementario (Supplementary Vocabulary)

tú, usted (you--int., for.)
Tú eres un buen hijo. (You are a good son.)
Usted es un buen médico. (You are a good doctor.)

tu, tus; su, sus (your--int., for.)
¿Preparas la mesa para tu mamá? (Do you prepare the table for your mom?)
¿Visitas a tus amigos en el verano? (Do you visit your friends in the summer?)

te, le (to you--int., for.). These object pronouns are used as indirect objects with the verbs _gustar_ (to please) and _doler_ (to hurt).
¿Te duelen mucho los dientes? (Do your teeth hurt much?)
¿Le gustan las hamburguesas? (Do you like hamburgers?)

tí (you). The stressed object pronoun of the second person singular intimate is introduced for use as the object of prepositions. _Usted_ is used for the formal.
El mono no quiere ir hacia tí. (The monkey doesn't want to go toward you.)
El plato blanco es para usted. (The white plate is for you.)

contigo (with you--int.)
Tu mamá va contigo a ver al médico. (Your mom is going with you to see the doctor.)

si (if). Since only the present indicative is used in both the if clause and the result clause, this conjunction is used to express simple conditions and expected results.
¿Vas al jardín zoológico si no llueve? (Are you going to the zoo if it doesn't rain?)
No voy a la escuela si tengo gripe. (I'm not going to school if I have the flu.)

cuando (when); mientras (que)(while). These adverbs use the present indicative and refer to situations regarded as facts.
Voy al dentista cuando me duelen los dientes. (I go to the dentist when my teeth hurt.)
Juan come el sandwich mientras que yo preparo la sopa. (John eats the sandwich while I prepare the soup.)

por (during, for; in; through, along)
¿Vas a la playa por una semana? (Are you going to the beach for a week?)
¿Va usted al parque por la tarde? (Do you go to the park in the afternoon?)
Paso por tu pueblo cuando regreso de Los Ángeles. (I pass through your town when I return from Los Angeles.)

para (destined for; to be used for)
La hamburguesa es para tí y el perro caliente es para mí. (The hamburger is for you and the hot dog is for me.)
Pon los vasos para la leche, por favor. (Put on the glasses for the milk, please.)

todavía (still, yet)
¿No vienes todavía? (Aren't you coming yet?)
Mi hermano no quiere venir todavía. (My brother doesn't want to come yet.)

ya (already, now, at once)
¿Ya estás aquí? (Are you here already?)
Ya vas a ver los elefantes. (Now you are going to see the elephants.)
¡Vas a la escuela ya! (You are going to school at once!)

seco, mojado (dry, wet); roto, sano (broken, sound); manso, feroz (tame, gentle; savage, ferocious). These adjectives, as in earlier levels, have opposite meanings.
¿Está seco tu paraguas? (Is your umbrella dry?)
Mi bicicleta está rota. (My bicycle is broken.)
El león es un animal feroz. (The lion is a ferocious animal.)

fuerte (hard, strong); suave (soft, gentle). When fuerte is used as in un dolor fuerte (a strong pain), suave has no contrasting meaning.
¿Es fuerte la lluvia? (Is it a hard rain?)
No estoy mojado porque la lluvia es suave. (I'm not wet because the rain is gentle.)
Tengo un dolor muy fuerte en la espalda. (I have a very strong pain in my back.)

mejor, peor (better, worse)
Tienes que ir al médico si te sientes peor hoy. (You have to go to the doctor if you feel worse today.)
¡Estoy mejor ahora! (I feel better now!)

(tener) miedo (to be frightened)
Jorge tiene miedo al médico. (George is frightened of the doctor.)

(el) inglés (English); (el) español (Spanish). The names of other languages can also be introduced if desired.
¿Por qué vas a la clase de español? (Why do you go to Spanish class?)
Voy porque me gusta hablar español. (I go because I like to speak Spanish.)

las vacaciones (vacation); la visita (visit, visitor)
Me voy a la playa para las vacaciones. (I'm going away to the beach for the vacation.)
¿Tienes visitas en casa? (Do you have visitors at your house?)

Vocabulario Básico (Basic Vocabulary)
    This level includes examples of themes instead of sentences. When dialogues and conversations are developed around themes, new words and expressions are taught as necessary for the creation of a natural flow of the language.

Los alimentos (Foods)

Nouns	Verbs			Modifiers
el almuerzo	comes	llevar	querer	los colores
el dulce	dibujas	pasas	sacas	los números
la gelatina	lavo	puedes	tienes	
la hamburguesa	lavas	pones	tener	
el helado	lava	prepara	tienes que	
la papa	lavar	preparas	tener que	
las papas fritas	llevo	prepara	tocas	
el perro caliente	llevas	preparar	ves	
el sandwich	lleva	quieres	ver	
la sopa				

Examples of themes

A child insists on typical lunch foods for breakfast.

Parents try to encourage their child to try other foods but the child wants
   to eat only french fries.

Los animales (Animals)

Nouns	Verbs			Modifiers
el camello	dibujas	jugar	ser	los colores
el elefante	entiende	lava	tienes	los números
la girafa	entender	lavar	tener	seco
el hipopótamo	escucho	lleva	tienes que	mojado
el león	escuchas	llevar	tener que	manso
el mono	escucha	pasas	tocas	feroz
el tigre	escuchar	poder	ves	fuerte
	habla	pones	ver	mejor
	ir	prepara	viene	peor
	se va	preparar	venir	
	irse	querer	visitas	
	juega	sacas	visitar	
			vivir	

Examples of themes

A sick animal is examined and treated by a veterinarian and helpers.

A child helps the caretaker feed the animals.

El calendario (Calendar)

Nouns	Verbs			Modifiers
el año	estás	llueve	vengo	mejor
la estación	hace	llover	vienes	peor
la primavera	vas	nieva	viene	
el verano	ir	nevar	venir	
el otoño	me voy	preparo	viajas	
el invierno	te vas	preparas	visito	
	se va	prepara	visitas	
	irse	preparar	visita	
	llevas	regresa	visitar	
	puesto			

Examples of themes

An adult discusses summer and winter vacation possibilities with a travel
   agent.

Friends visiting from a warm climate enjoy their first experience with snow.

La casa (House)

Nouns	Verbs			Modifiers
la cuchara	abres	ir	preparas	los colores
el cuchillo	abrir	lavo	prepara	los números
el horno	ayudas	lavas	preparar	seco
la mesa	bebes	lava	quieres	mojado
el plato	cierras	lavar	querer	roto
el refrigerador	cerrar	llevo	sacas	sano
la silla	comes	llevas	tienes	mejor
la taza	dibujas	lleva	tener	peor
el tenedor	escucho	llevar	tienes que	
el vaso	escuchas	pasas	tener que	
	escucha	puedes	tiras	
	escuchar	poder	tocas	
	vas	pones	ves	
		preparo	ver	

Examples of themes

Just as a visitor is about to come for lunch, the oven overheats and burns
   the food.

Children prepare a surprise breakfast for Mother's Day with considerable
   difficulty.

La ciudad (City)

Nouns	Verbs			Modifiers
la acera	caminas	llover	tener que	los números
la calle	corres	nieva	tiras	seco
la ciudad	dibujas	nevar	tocas	mojado
el jardín	estás	pasas	vengo	roto
zoológico	vas	puedes	vienes	mejor
el parque	ir	poder	viene	peor
el pueblo	me voy	pones	venir	
	te vas	quieres	ves	
	se va	querer	ver	
	irse	regresas	viajas	
	juego	sacas	visito	
	juegas	saltas	visitas	
	juega	tienes	visita	
	jugar	tener	visitar	
	llueve	tienes que	vives	
			vivir	

Examples of themes

Travelers search for a friend's house but discover finally that they are
   looking in the wrong town.

A lonely lion escapes from the zoo and searches for someone to be his
   friend.

El clima (Climate)

Nouns	Verbs			Modifiers
(hace) calor	caminas	llevas	saltas	fuerte
(hace) fresco	corres	puesto	tocas	suave
(hace) frío	estás	llueve	tienes	mejor
la lluvia	hace	llover	tener	peor
la nieve	vas	nieva	tener que	
el sol	ir	nevar	vengo	
el tiempo	juego	puedes	vienes	
	juegas	poder	viene	
	juega	quieres	venir	
	jugar	querer	ves	
		regresas	ver	

Examples of themes
A child insists on wearing summer clothing in the winter.
A family on a picnic is drenched in a heavy rain.

El cuerpo humano (Body parts)

Nouns	Verbs			Modifiers
la espalda	dibujas	lava	tienes	los números
el diente	lavo	lavar	tener	seco
la garganta	lavas	tocas	ves	mojado
el vientre			ver	roto
				sano
				mejor
				peor

Examples of themes
A child tries to convince parents that he/she is sick and should not go to
  school.
A Spanish speaking doctor and nurse try to discover the illness of a traveler who does not speak the language.

La escuela (School)
Children like to say what grade they are in, so the ordinal numbers that
correspond to the grades of the children in the class are taught.

Nouns	Verbs			Modifiers
la clase	escucho	regresas	viene	los números
el grado	escuchas	ser	venir	roto
el timbre	escucha	tienes	ves	sano
	escuchar	tener	ver	fuerte
	estás	tienes que	visito	suave
	vas	tener que	visitas	mejor
	ir	vengo	visita	peor
		vienes	visitar	

Examples of themes
A pet monkey escapes from a cage at school and cannot be found.
Identical twins exchange places in school and create confusion.

La familia (Family)

Nouns		Verbs		Modifiers
la hija	ayudas	juego	quiere	los números
el hijo	dibujas	juegas	querer	seco
	entiendo	juega	sacas	mojado
	entiendes	jugar	se siente	sano
	entiende	lavo	ser	mejor
	entender	lavas	tienes	peor
	estás	lava	tener	
	estudia	lavar	tienes que	
	estudiar	te llamas	tener que	
	escucho	llevo	viene	
	escuchas	llevas	vienes	
	escucha	lleva	venir	
	escuchar	llevar	ves	
	hablo	puedes	ver	
	hablas	poder	viajas	
	habla	preparo	visito	
	hablar	preparas	visitas	
	ir	prepara	visita	
	se va	preparar	visitar	
	irse	quieres	vivir	

No themes are listed for this vocabulary area because these words represent roles that are integrated into the themes of other vocabulary areas.

La hora (Time)

Nouns
These words are used to indicate when an action takes place; they combine with all the action verbs.

la mañana
la noche
la tarde

Examples of themes
An exhausted bus tells its bus companions what it does through each part of
  the day to make it so tired.
A child and parent argue about when to have the child's birthday party--the
  child wants it at night; the parent, in the afternoon.

La naturaleza (Nature)

Nouns		Verbs		Modifiers
la arena	caminas	llevas	tienes	los colores
el barro	corres	lleva	tener	los números
el desierto	dibujas	llevar	tienes que	seco
la playa	estás	llueve	tener que	mojado
el río	estudio	llover	tiras	mejor
la selva	estudias	nieva	tocas	peor
	estudia	nevar	vengo	
	estudiar	puedes	vienes	

hace	poder	viene
vas	preparo	venir
ir	preparas	ves
me voy	prepara	ver
te vas	preparar	viajas
se va	quieres	visito
juegas	querer	visitas
juega	regresas	visita
jugar	sacas	visitar
llevo	saltas	vives
		vivir

Examples of themes
Mother hippopotamus teaches her child to play in the mud.
An unruly camel becomes a hero when it leads thirsty travelers to an oasis.

Las profesiones (Professions)

Nouns	Verbs			Modifiers
el dentista	abrir	hablar	querer	los números
el enfermero	cerrar	ir	ser	mejor
el médico	entiendo	lava	tener	peor
el paciente	entiende	lavar	tener que	
el policía	entender	lleva	viene	
	hablo	llevar	venir	
	habla	poder	ver	
			vivir	

Examples of themes
Dentist and parent try to convince a young child to open his/her mouth for a
   dental examination.
A big eater whose stomach hurts seeks advice from a doctor.

La ropa (Clothing)

Nouns	Verbs			Modifiers
la bufanda	abres	lavas	quieres	los colores
la chaqueta	abrir	lava	querer	los números
el gorro	cierras	lavar	tienes	seco
el guante	cerrar	llevo	tener	mojado
el impermeable	dibujas	llevas	tienes que	roto
el paraguas	vas	lleva	tener que	sano
el sombrero	ir	llevar	tiras	mejor
	juego	llevas	tocas	peor
	juegas	puesto	viene	
	juega	pasas	venir	
	jugar	puedes	ves	
	lavo	poder	ver	

Examples of themes
Father wants a hat for his birthday and every package he opens contains one.
While shopping for a jacket for the child, the child decides on one, the
   mother prefers another, and the father still another.

El transporte (Transportation)

Nouns	Verbs			Modifiers
el autobús	dibujas	lavo	ser	los colores
el taxi	estás	lavas	tienes	los números
el tren	escucho	lava	tener	seco
	escuchas	lavar	tienes que	mojado
	escucha	lleva	tener que	roto
	escuchar	llevar	tocas	sano
	vas	pasas	vengo	mejor
	ir	puedes	vienes	peor
	juego	poder	viene	
	juegas	quieres	venir	
	juega	querer	ves	
	jugar	regresas	ver	
		sacas	viajas	

Examples of themes
Several children compare their collections of toy vehicles.
A child and a parent take a broken toy train to a repair shop to be fixed.

V O C A B U L A R Y

Los Verbos*

abres	ir	preparar
abrir	me voy	quieres
ayudas	te vas	querer
bebes	se va	regresas
caminas	irse	sacas
cierras	juego	saltas
cerrar	juegas	me siento
comes	juega	te sientes
corres	jugar	se siente
dibujas	lavo	eres
entiendo	lavas	ser
entiendes	lava	tienes
entiende	lavar	tener
entender	te llamas	tienes que
escucho	llevo	tener que
escuchas	llevas	tiras
escucha	lleva	tocas
escuchar	llevar	vengo
estás	llevas puesto	vienes
estudio	llueve	viene
estudias	llover	venir
estudia	nieva	ves
estudiar	nevar	ver
hablo	pasas	viajas
hablas	puedes	visito
habla	poder	visitas
hablar	pones	visita
hace	preparo	visitar
vas	preparas	vives
	prepara	vivir

---

*Each verb given in the second person intimate is also taught in the second person formal.

Vocabulario Básico

Los alimentos
el almuerzo
el dulce
la gelatina
la hamburguesa
el helado
la papa
las papas fritas
el perro caliente
el sandwich
la sopa

Los animales
el camello
el elefante
la girafa
el hipopótamo
el león
el mono
el tigre

El calendario
el año
la estación
la primavera
el verano
el otoño
el invierno

La casa
la cuchara
el cuchillo
el horno
la mesa
el plato
el refrigerador
la silla
la taza
el tenedor
el vaso

La ciudad
la acera
la calle
la ciudad
el jardín zoológico
el parque
el pueblo

El clima
(hace) calor
(hace) fresco
(hace) frío
la lluvia
la nieve
el sol
el tiempo

Los colores
azul celeste
gris
rosado

El cuerpo humano
la espalda
el diente
la garganta
el vientre

La escuela
la clase
el grado
el timbre

La familia
la hija
el hijo

La hora
la mañana
la noche
la tarde

La naturaleza
la arena
el barro
el desierto
la playa
el río
la selva

Los numeros
51–100

Las profesiones
el dentista
el enfermero
el médico
el paciente
el policía

La ropa
la bufanda
la chaqueta
el gorro
el guante
el impermeable
el paraguas
el sombrero

Transporte
el autobús
el taxi
el tren

Oraciones Interrogativas
¿Cuál es (tu dirección)?
¿Cuándo (te vas de
  vacaciones)?

Expresiones Comunes
¿Cómo está usted?
Me siento (mejor).
¡Hola!
¿Qué tal?
¡Qué lluvia tan fuerte!
¡Qué animal feroz!

52

Vocabulario Suplementario

tú	mientras (que)	feroz
usted	por	fuerte
tu, tus	para	suave
su, sus	todavía	mejor
te	ya	peor
le	seco	(tener) miedo
tí	mojado	(el) inglés
contigo	roto	(el) español
si	sano	las vacaciones
cuando	manso	la visita

LEVEL 5

In this level the plural forms of the verbs are taught: the <u>nosotros</u>, <u>nosotras</u> (we) form: first person plural; the <u>ustedes</u> (you) form: second person plural; and the <u>ellos</u>, <u>ellas</u> (they) form: third person plural. <u>Ustedes</u> is used for both the second person intimate and formal as is common usage in conversation in the majority of Spanish speaking countries.

Descriptions are used for introducing the plural verb forms; then dialogues and conversations are developed employing both the singular and the plural forms. The new vocabulary of this level has been chosen to stimulate ideas for dialogues and conversations—for example, shopping scenes and radio or television programs.

The third person plural is first used in describing actions that the children see pictured in illustrations or films or hear about in stories or songs. To introduce the third person plural, the teacher models the statement and the children repeat it. When they become familiar with the new verb forms, the children describe the actions themselves; for example:

Los niños miran el programa de televisión. (The children watch the television program.

Los perros juegan con la pelota. (The dogs play with the ball.)
Los osos caminan por el bosque. (The bears walk in the woods.)
Las ovejas tienen hambre y frío. (The sheep are hungry and cold.)

For further practice, these verbs can be used in new situations. For example, children can describe what their classmates, who are pantomiming these actions, are doing.

Ellos miran un libro. (They look at a book.)
Ellas juegan con el gato. (They play with the cat.)
Ellos caminan hacia la puerta. (They walk toward the door.)
Ellas tienen los dulces. (They have the candy.)

The third person plural can also be used to describe groupings such as <u>las escuelas</u> (schools), <u>los árboles</u> (trees), <u>los elefantes</u> (elephants). In making these descriptions, the children express all the information they can about the subject; for example:

Los elefantes son animales muy grandes. (Elephants are very large animals.)
Viven en las selvas. (They live in jungles.)
A ellos les gusta jugar en el barro y el agua. (They like to play in the mud and the water.)

53

From the descriptions that have been made in previous levels, the chil--
dren will be able to describe such groupings as sus padres (his parents), mis
hermanos (my brothers), tus primos (your cousins). For example:
  Tus primos viven en México. (Your cousins live in Mexico.)
  Vienen aquí el año que viene. (They are coming here next year.)
  No hablan inglés, hablan español. (They don't speak English, they speak
Spanish.)

The first person plural is introduced as the teacher describes what they
are doing together as a group. The teacher can describe what they are actually doing or what they are pantomiming. The children practice the first person
plural by first repeating what the teacher says and then making their own sentences with the familiar verb forms.

  Escuchamos el disco nuevo. (We listen to the new record.)
  Llevamos puestos los zapatos. (We are wearing shoes.)
  Jugamos con la pelota. (We are playing with the ball.)

The nosotros (we) form can also be used as the children describe them-
selves as a group.
  Vivimos en una ciudad grande. (We live in a large city.)
  Estamos en quinto grado. (We are in fifth grade.)
  Estudiamos español los lunes, miércoles, y viernes. (We study Spanish on
Monday, Wednesday, and Friday.)
  Nos gusta comer las hamburguesas y las papas fritas. (We like to eat ham-
burgers and french fries.)

The first and third persons plural can be used together and contrasted by
dividing the group into two parts and having an observer and member of one of
the groups describe and contrast the groups, nosotros (we) and ellos, ellas
(they); for example:

  Nosotros llevamos puestas las botas y ellos llevan puestos los zapatos. (We
are wearing boots and they are wearing shoes.)
  Nosotros dibujamos con tizas y ellas dibujan con lápices. (We draw with
chalk and they draw with pencils.)

The second person plural, ustedes (you), is taught after the third person
plural has been mastered, because the verb form used with the second person
plural is identical to that used with the third person plural. In learning
to use the second person plural form, ustedes (you), the children are learning
a new use for a familiar verb form.
  After the second person plural has been introduced, dialogues can be developed that employ the plural. Characters in the dialogues can now represent
groups rather than individuals, for example: students, parents, cousins,
friends. The following example is a dialogue between brothers and sisters:

  Juan: ¿Adónde van ustedes? (Where are you going?)
  María: Vamos a regresar a casa. Vienen con nosotros? (We are going to return home. Are you coming with us?)
  Juan: No, no estoy listo para regresar a casa. Jorge y Jaime, ¿ustedes
quieren regresar ahora? (No, I'm not ready to return home. George and Jim,
do you want to return now?)
  Jorge: No, no quiero ir todavía. (No, I don't want to go yet.)

Jaime: Sí, quiero irme. Ya me voy. (Yes, I want to go. I'm going now.)
María: Bueno, nos vamos ya. ¡Adiós! (Well, we're going now. Good-bye!)
Jorge y Juan: ¡Adiós! (Good-bye!)

S E L E C T I O N   A N D   U S E   O F   V O C A B U L A R Y

Los Verbos (Verbs)

The new verbs of this level are used with the new vocabulary in developing dialogues and conversations. Their usage is illustrated here.

compro, compras, compra, compramos, compran, comprar (to buy); cuesta, cuestan (to cost); hago, haces, hacemos, hacen, hacer (compras) (to do shopping); pago, pagas, paga, pagamos, pagan, pagar (to pay); vendo, vendes, vende, vendemos, venden, vender (to sell)
Queremos comprar el radio pero es muy caro. (We want to buy the radio but it is very expensive.)
¿Cuánto cuesta esta cartera? (How much does this purse cost?)
Hacen sus compras los sábados. (They do their shopping on Saturdays.)
¿Quién va a pagar? (Who is going to pay?)
¿Vende usted este sofá a un precio rebajado? (Are you selling this sofa at a reduced price?)

duermo, duermes, duerme, dormimos, duermen, dormir (to sleep)
Tengo mucho sueño y quiero ir a dormir ahora. (I am very sleepy and I want to go to sleep now.)
Ellos no duermen bien en esta cama. (They don't sleep well in this bed.)

miro, miras, mira, miramos, miran, mirar (look at, watch)
Queremos mirar las noticias en el televisor. (We want to watch the news on television.)
No me gusta mirar este programa. (I don't like to watch this program.)

Oraciones Interrogativas (Interrogative Sentences)

Two of the interrogative sentences taught in this level are related to shopping: ¿Cuánto cuesta (la cartera)? (How much is [the purse]?) ¿De qué talla es (el vestido)? (What size is [the dress]?) Other questions that can be used when shopping are added so that the children are able to make a natural conversational exchange when dramatizing the roles of clerk and customer.

The third interrogative sentence is: ¿Cuál es la fecha? (What is the date?) Children can now answer with the month and year: La fecha es el treinta de enero de mil novecientos ochenta y dos. (The date is the thirtieth of January, nineteen eighty-two.)

Vocabulario Suplementario (Supplementary Vocabulary)

nosotros, nosotras (we--m., f., subject; us, object of preposition); ustedes (you--subject, object of preposition); ellos, ellas (they--m., f., subject; them, object of preposition). Subject pronouns are omitted except when they are needed for emphasis or clarification.
Nosotros no vamos al supermercado. ¡Ustedes tienen que ir! (We are not going to the supermarket. You have to go!)
Ellos miran el programa en el televisor mientras preparan la cena. (They watch the program on television while they prepare the supper.)
¿Tienes unas monedas para nosotros? (Do you have some coins for us?)

¿Quién viene con ustedes? (Who is coming with you?)
Las flores son de ellas. (The flowers are from them.)

nuestro, nuestros; nuestra, nuestras (our--m., f.); su, sus (your, their)
Nuestra tía es muy rica. (Our aunt is very rich.)
No veo nuestras carteras en la sala. (I don't see our purses in the living
room.)
Sus gafas están muy sucias. (Your eyeglasses are very dirty.)

nos (to us); les (to you). These object pronouns are used as indirect
objects with the verbs gustar (to please) and doler (to hurt).
Nos duelen los pies porque caminamos demasiado. (Our feet hurt because we
are walking too much.)
¿Les gusta mi disco nuevo? (Do you like my new record?)

alto, bajo (tall, short); rico, pobre (rich, poor); caro, barato (expensive, cheap); enfermo, sano (sick, healthy); apagado, encendido (turned off,
turned on); rabajado (reduced, lowered); aumentado (increased, raised). Opposites are taught together and contrasted.
Este espejo es demasiado alto para mi hermano. (This mirror is too high for
my brother.)
No tienen un tío rico. (They don't have a rich uncle.)
No queremos comprar una frazada barata. (We don't want to buy a cheap blanket.)
La luz de la sala está apagada. (The living room light is turned off.)
Compramos esta alfombra porque el precio está rebajado. (We are buying this
rug because the price is reduced.)

demasiado, (too, followed by an adjective or adverb; too much--s.; too
many--pl.)
Ella es demasiada bonita. (She is too pretty.)
No quiero esta blusa porque está demasiada sucia. (I don't want this blouse
because it is too dirty.)
Tenemos demasiados tenedores. (We have too many forks.)

suficiente (sufficient, enough)
Tenemos suficientes frazadas ya. (We have sufficient blankets now.)
No tengo suficiente dinero para comprar este cinturón. (I don't have enough
money to buy this belt.)

juntos (together)
¿Vamos juntos al cine? (Are we going together to the cinema?)

el cambio (change); el dinero (money); la moneda (coin); el paquete
(package); el precio (price); (ir de) compras (to go shopping); (hacer) com-
pras (to do the shopping)
No tenemos nada de cambio. (We don't have any change.)
Tenemos mucho dinero pero es todo en monedas. (We have a lot of money but
it is all in coins.)
Nosotros podemos llevar los paquetes. (We can carry the packages.)
Los precios están rebajados en aquella tienda. (The prices are reduced in
that shop.)
Vamos a ir de compras juntos. (We are going shopping together.)
Ellos hacen sus compras muy temprano por la mañana. (They do their shopping
very early in the morning.)

el dolor (pain); la gripe (flu); la medicina (medicine); el resfriado
(cold)
   Tengo un dolor fuerte de cabeza. (I have a bad headache.)
   Mis hermanos tienen gripe. (My brothers have the flu.)
   Tienen que tomar la medicina para el resfriado. (They have to take the med-
icine for colds.)

Vocabulario Básico (Basic Vocabulary)

Los alimentos (Foods)

Nouns	Verbs			Modifiers
la carne de vaca	abrimos	hacer	preparan	los colores
la cena	abren	van	queremos	los números
el flan	bebemos	llevamos	quieren	rico
la lechuga	beben	llevan	sacamos	caro
el maíz	comemos	miro	sacan	barato
el melón	comen	miras	son	rebajado
el pescado	compro	mira	tenemos	aumentado
el pollo	compras	miramos	tienen	demasiado
el tomate	compra	miran	tenemos que	suficiente
la torta	compramos	mirar	tienen que	juntos
las uvas	compran	pago	tocamos	
la zanahoria	comprar	pagas	tocan	
	cuesta	paga	vendo	
	cuestan	pagamos	vendes	
	dibujamos	pagan	vende	
	dibujan	pagar	vendemos	
	están	podemos	venden	
	hago	pueden	vender	
	haces	ponemos	vemos	
	hacemos	ponen	ven	
	hacen	preparamos		

Examples of themes
A child's tomato plant produces melon-sized tomatoes that astonish everyone
   and make the child famous.
Mrs. Rabbit's bunnies eat too much lettuce and too many carrots and become
   ill.

Los animales (Animals)

Nouns	Verbs			Modifiers
la ardilla	ayudamos	hablan	sacamos	los colores
el ciervo	ayudan	hacen	sacan	los números
el conejo	beben	van	saltan	caro
el lobo	caminan	se van	son	barato
el oso	comemos	jugamos	tenemos	enfermo
el pájaro	comen	juegan	tienen	sano
la serpiente	compro	se llaman	tiran	rebajado
el zorro	compras	miro	tocamos	aumentado
	compra	miras	tocan	demasiado
	compramos	mira	vendo	suficiente
	compran	miramos	vendes	juntos

comprar	miran	vende
corren	mirar	vendemos
cuesta	pasamos	venden
cuestan	pasan	vender
dibujamos	pueden	vemos
dibujan	ponemos	ven
duermen	ponen	visitamos
entendemos	preparan	visitan
entienden	queremos	vivimos
están	quieren	viven
hablamos	regresan	

Examples of themes

A family or group of animals is personified in any situation. For example,
a family of bears catches fish in a stream for their meal, but the baby
bear prefers playing in the water to helping; or the fox brings home his
catch to a hungry family. (When animals are personified the above verb
list will expand considerably.)

Familiar folk tales and fables involving animals can be varied to provide
use of the plural. For example, instead of Little Red Riding Hood visiting her grandmother, two sisters visit their grandparents.

El calendario (Calendar)

This vocabulary is used in telling the date and in placing an event in
time. The thoughts expressed with these words must be in the present tense.
This vocabulary is used in the themes of other vocabulary areas.

Nouns

la fecha	enero	abril	julio	octubre
el mes	febrero	mayo	agosto	noviembre
	marzo	junio	septiembre	diciembre

La casa (House)

Nouns	Verbs			Modifiers
la alfombra	compro	llevan	queremos	los colores
la almohada	compras	miro	quieren	los números
la cama	compra	miras	sacamos	alto
la cómoda	compramos	mira	sacan	bajo
el espejo	compran	miramos	son	caro
la frazada	comprar	miran	tenemos	barato
la lámpara	cuesta	mirar	tienen	apagado
la luz	cuestan	pago	tenemos que	encendido
el sillón	dibujamos	pagas	tienen que	rebajado
el sofá	dibujan	paga	tiramos	aumentado
	dormimos	pagamos	tiran	demasiado
	duermen	pagan	tocamos	suficiente
	escuchamos	pagar	tocan	juntos
	escuchan	pasamos	vendo	
	estamos	pasan	vendes	
	están	podemos	vende	
	jugamos	pueden	vendemos	
	juegan	ponemos	venden	
	lavamos	ponen	vender	
	lavan	preparamos	vemos	
	llevamos	preparan	ven	

Examples of themes

Brothers and sisters can't agree on which lamp to buy their mother for her birthday.

Cousins who are spending the night together hear strange noises and see strange things.

La ciudad (City)

Nouns	Verbs			Modifiers
el cine	caminamos	vamos	tienen	los colores
el hospital	caminan	van	tenemos que	los números
la iglesia	comemos	nos vamos	tienen que	alto
el supermercado	comen	se van	vendo	bajo
la tienda	compro	miro	vendes	caro
	compras	miras	vende	barato
	compra	mira	vendemos	demasiado
	compramos	miramos	venden	suficiente
	compran	miran	vender	juntos
	comprar	mirar	venimos	
	corremos	podemos	vienen	
	corren	pueden	vemos	
	dibujamos	queremos	ven	
	dibujan	quieren	visitamos	
	dormimos	regresamos	visitan	
	duermen	regresan	vivimos	
	estamos	son	viven	
	están	tenemos		

Examples of themes

A storm cuts out the lights in a supermarket and two shoppers try to find the fruits and vegetables they need by the sense of touch.

The children's rich uncle buys a cinema just for them and their friends.

El clima (Climate)

Nouns	Verbs			Modifiers
el hielo	caminamos	miro	sacamos	los colores
la nube	caminan	miras	sacan	los números
la tormenta	corremos	mira	saltamos	alto
el viento	corren	miramos	saltan	bajo
	escuchamos	miran	son	demasiado
	escuchan	mirar	tenemos	suficiente
	estamos	podemos	tienen	juntos
	están	pueden	tiramos	
	estudiamos	ponemos	tiran	
	estudian	ponen	tocamos	
	jugamos	queremos	tocan	
	juegan	quieren	vemos	
	llevamos	regresamos	ven	
	llevan	regresan	viajamos	
			viajan	

Examples of themes

As the winds and storms of winter come, the bear family prepares for their long winter nap.

Things begin blowing away at an outdoor birthday party when a strong wind
develops.

La comunicación (Communication)

Nouns	Verbs			Modifiers
el disco	compro	miras	sacamos	los números
la música	compras	mira	sacan	caro
las noticias	compra	miramos	son	barato
el programa	compramos	miran	tenemos	rebajado
la propaganda	compran	mirar	tienen	aumentado
el radio	comprar	pago	tenemos que	apagado
el televisor	cuesta	pagas	tienen que	encendido
la televisión	cuestan	paga	tocamos	demasiado
el tocadiscos	entendemos	pagamos	tocan	suficiente
	entienden	pagan	vendo	juntos
	escuchamos	pagar	vendes	
	escuchan	podemos	vende	
	están	pueden	vendemos	
	hablan	ponemos	venden	
	llevamos	ponen	vender	
	llevan	queremos	vemos	
	miro	quieren	ven	

Examples of themes

Radio and television shows and advertisements can be created around other
vocabulary, for example, a weather report, advertising for a fantastic
sale at a women's clothing store.

La familia (Family)

Nouns	Verbs			Modifiers
la prima	abren	hacer	quieren	alto
el primo	ayudan	van	regresan	bajo
la tía	beben	se van	sacan	rico
el tío	caminan	juegan	saltan	pobre
	cierran	lavan	se sienten	enfermo
	comen	se llaman	son	sano
	compra	llevan	tienen	demasiado
	compran	llevan puestos	tienen que	suficiente
	comprar	mira	tiran	juntos
	corren	miran	tocan	
	duerme	mirar	vende	
	duermen	paga	venden	
	dormir	pagan	vender	
	entienden	pagar	vienen	
	escuchan	pasan	ven	
	están	pueden	viajan	
	estudian	ponen	visitan	
	hablan	preparan	viven	
	hacen			

These vocabulary words are integrated into the themes of other vocabulary
areas.

Las profesiones (Professions)

Nouns	Verbs			Modifiers
el anunciador	ayudamos	hacer	ponen	los números
el cantante	ayudan	van	preparan	alto
el dependiente	beben	se van	queremos	bajo
el reportero	caminan	juegan	quieren	pobre
	comen	lavan	regresan	rico
	compra	se llaman	sacan	enfermo
	compran	llevan	saltan	sano
	comprar	llevan puestos	somos	juntos
	contestamos	miro	son	
	contestan	miras	tienen	
	corren	mira	tienen que	
	duermen	miramos	tiran	
	entendemos	miran	tocan	
	entienden	mirar	vende	
	escuchamos	pago	venden	
	escuchan	pagas	vender	
	están	paga	vienen	
	estudiamos	pagamos	vemos	
	estudian	pagan	ven	
	hablamos	pagar	viajan	
	hablan	pasan	visitan	
	hacen	pueden	viven	

Examples of themes

A newscaster doesn't prepare the news well and makes ridiculous errors.
On the night of the program, the singer has a very sore throat and loses
   his/her voice.

La ropa (Clothing)

Nouns	Verbs			Modifiers
la bolsa	abrimos	llevan	sacan	los colores
la cartera	abren	puestos	son	los números
el cinturón	compro	miro	tenemos	caro
las gafas	compras	miras	tienen	barato
la talla	compra	mira	tenemos que	rebajado
	compramos	miramos	tienen que	demasiado
	compran	miran	tiramos	suficiente
	comprar	mirar	tiran	juntos
	cuesta	pago	tocamos	
	cuestan	pagas	tocan	
	dibujamos	paga	vendo	
	dibujan	pagamos	vendes	
	están	pagan	vende	
	jugamos	pagar	vendemos	
	juegan	podemos	venden	
	llevamos	pueden	vemos	
	llevan	queremos	ven	
	llevamos	quieren		
	puestos	sacamos		

Examples of themes
A clerk tries to help a woman who can't decide which of many purses to buy.
Just as he is about to leave on an important business trip, Father can't
    find his eyeglasses.

V O C A B U L A R Y

Los Verbos

abrimos	hablan	preparamos
abren	hago	preparan
ayudamos	haces	queremos
ayudan	hacemos	quieren
bebemos	hacen	regresamos
beben	hacer	regresan
caminamos	vamos	sacamos
caminan	van	sacan
cerramos	nos vamos	saltamos
cierran	se van	saltan
comemos	jugamos	nos sentimos
comen	juegan	se sienten
compro	lavamos	somos
compras	lavan	son
compra	nos llamamos	tenemos
compramos	se llaman	tienen
compran	llevamos	tenemos que
comprar	llevan	tienen que
corremos	llevamos puestos	tiramos
corren	llevan puestos	tiran
cuesta	miro	tocamos
cuestan	miras	tocan
dibujamos	mira	vendo
dibujan	miramos	vendes
duermo	miran	vende
duermes	mirar	vendemos
duerme	pago	venden
dormimos	pagas	vender
duermen	paga	venimos
dormir	pagamos	vienen
entendemos	pagan	vemos
entienden	pagar	ven
escuchamos	pasamos	viajamos
escuchan	pasan	viajan
estamos	podemos	visitamos
están	pueden	visitan
estudiamos	ponemos	vivimos
estudian	ponen	viven
hablamos		

Vocabulario Básico

Los alimentos

la carne de vaca	el maíz	el tomate
la cena	el melón	la torta
el flan	el pescado	las uvas
la lechuga	el pollo	la zanahoria

Los animales
la ardilla
el ciervo
el conejo
el lobo
el oso
el pájaro
la serpiente
el zorro

El calendario
la fecha
el mes
enero
febrero
marzo
abril
mayo
junio
julio
agosto
septiembre
octubre
noviembre
diciembre

La casa
la alfombra
la almohada
la cama
la cómoda
el espejo
la frazada
la lámpara
la luz
el sillón
el sofá

La ciudad
el cine
el hospital
la iglesia
el supermercado
la tienda

El clima
el hielo
la nube
la tormenta
el viento

La comunicación
el disco
la música
las noticias
el programa
la propaganda
el radio
la televisión
el televisor
el tocadiscos

La familia
la prima
el primo
la tía
el tío

Los números
101-10,000

Las profesiones
el anunciador
el cantante
el dependiente
el reportero

La ropa
la bolsa
la cartera
el cinturón
las gafas
la talla

Oraciones Interrogativas
¿Cuánto cuesta (la cartera)?
¿De qué talla es (el vestido)?
¿Cuál es la fecha?

Vocabulario Suplementario

nosotros, nosotras
ustedes
ellos, ellas
nuestro, nuestros
nuestra, nuestras
su, sus
nos
les
alto
bajo
rico
pobre

caro
barato
enfermo
sano
apagado
encendido
rebajado
aumentado
demasiado
suficiente
juntos

el cambio
el dinero
la moneda
el paquete
el precio
(ir de) compras
(hacer) compras
el dolor
la gripe
la medicina
el resfriado

LEVEL 6

The final level of the curriculum has three equally important facets. *The first* is greater emphasis on conversation. Dialogues are still used in this level, especially in practicing the new vocabulary and verbs and in exploring the topic of travel, but conversations are developed more extensively than in previous levels. Some of these themes are to be developed only in conversations. The children should be encouraged to suggest additional topics in which they have particular interest.

When a theme or topic has been chosen, conversation partners are selected by either the teacher or the children. Without further preparation the children participate in short conversations with their partners. The group then reunites, and children who want to "replay" their conversation in front of the group are selected and the conversation is reenacted.

While not all partners can share their conversations each time, they should be encouraged to comment on anything that was of special interest to them. The children will see that each topic is developed somewhat differently by each set of partners and will begin to appreciate the diverse thoughts that can be expressed on a particular topic and the variety of ways they can be expressed.

As children take part in these spontaneous conversations, it is essential that the teacher understand it is more important for the children to develop confidence in speaking spontaneously than to speak with grammatical perfection. The teacher needs to create a supportive classroom atmosphere that encourages the children's participation. As they develop the necessary confidence they can gradually be made aware of errors they are making.

When the children have had extensive practice in participating in conversations, it is a good experience for them to converse with a native speaker if possible. The children and the native speaker both may feel more comfortable if they can converse informally while participating in a project or activity. For example, the children might help the speaker prepare a special native food for the class.

Meeting with the native speaker outside of class time is another way to expand the children's experience with the language. Part of the group might accompany a native speaker who is shopping for the family in the supermarket or go with a Spanish speaking family on an outing to a park. Some children will especially enjoy relating to very young children who are Spanish speakers and may feel more comfortable talking with them than with adults initially. If the group is divided, the ones who participated can share the experience with the rest of the group so that all can learn.

The children should know that they may not understand everything the na-

tive speaker says even though the teacher helps the native speaker realize beforehand what level of ability the children have attained. The children need
to practice making intelligent guesses about the meaning of words and phrases
that they have not studied and should ask for an explanation in Spanish if
they do not understand what is said. All the communication with the native
speaker should be in Spanish.

Children should have opportunities to converse with native speakers while
they are still in Spanish class and can share their experiences and receive
support from their teacher and companions. Having had these experiences, they
will be more likely to converse with Spanish speakers at other times and in
other situations.

The second important facet is the transition from this program to other
programs in which the children will continue their study of the language.
This transition is a concern of primary importance, because if it is not carefully planned the children may not continue their study.

Efforts should be concentrated on facilitating the transition with (1)
the administrators and the teaching staff of the new programs and (2) the
children and their parents. Good lines of communication should be established
with teachers and administrators who need to understand the importance of the
transition. The teachers can familiarize themselves with the objectives and
methodology of both programs and together develop a smooth transition for the
children. It will no doubt require the teachers of this program to incorpo-
rate other methodology and learning into their material to prepare the children for the upcoming program. At the same time, it would be helpful if the
teachers of the upcoming program adapt their material to build on the knowl-
edge and experiences the children already have. When the content and methodology of both programs have been revised to provide for a smooth passage, an
important obstacle will have been overcome.

Another important factor is the scheduling of the foreign language
classes in the middle school. Even children who have studied a foreign language throughout the elementary school years may not want to continue if they
must choose between foreign language and another essential skill, such as typ-
ing. Every effort should be made to provide scheduling that allows children
to take foreign language classes when desired.

The second area in which efforts can be concentrated is with the children
themselves and their parents. Both need to appreciate the value of learning
another language. They need to recognize the skill in conversation that the
children have developed and the importance of learning to read and write the
language. They also need to be assured that the upcoming program will build
on the skills they have already developed.

A practical use for the language in the near future is one of the best
motivations for the development of skill in a language. High schools that
make travel to a Spanish speaking country an opportunity available to advanced
language students provide tremendous incentive for the students. If such an
opportunity is not part of the high school program, it would be wise to work
with the staff of the middle school and the high school to provide it.

The third facet also will help motivate the children to continue their
study and provide themes for dialogues and conversations. It is the enrich-
ment of the children's understanding of Spanish speaking people and Latin culture. The focus of this study is travel. Traveling to another country and
experiencing with an open mind the realities of another culture are good ways
to gain an understanding and an appreciation of that culture. Although an actual trip may not be feasible immediately, the closer the children can come to
experiencing the realities of a trip the more meaningful this experience will
be for them.

The best way of introducing the children to this area is to invite several enthusiastic participants from the high school Spanish students' trip
abroad to share their experiences with the children. If this is not possible,
a native of or someone who has traveled or lived in a Latin country can be in-
vited. Whoever comes should be able to relate well to the children and stimulate their interest in these countries and cultures. By hearing firsthand
about travel to these countries, children will begin to imagine the possibility of travel for themselves.

When enthusiasm is generated, a country in which the children as a group
are interested in exploring is chosen. As the children become familiar with
that country a specific city or region is selected for in-depth study.

The preparations necessary for the trip are examined: visiting a travel
agency, getting vaccinations, acquiring passports, and packing suitcases. A
small group of children accompanied by the teacher might visit a local travel
agency (arrangements having been made beforehand) to learn about travel possibilities to the region or city that they have chosen to study. Pamphlets from
the travel agency can be shared with the other class members as modes of
transportation and lodging are discussed and "decided on."

Special excursions, festivals, museums, restaurants, and shopping expedi-
tions in that region or city are explored from the children's viewpoint as
travelers. Topics that have captured the children's interest are used as dialogue and conversation themes. A possible theme might focus on a child who
refuses to try any new foods while traveling and insists on only hamburgers
and french fries.

Treating these topics in dialogues and conversations will help children
relate to them on a personal level. It will encourage children to move be-
yond facts and begin to deal with feelings that arise when they are confronted
with a life style and culture different from their own. By discovering real
differences between their culture and a Latin culture, children will be ready
to explore why these differences exist--the historical background of the two
cultures. An understanding of the differences between cultures and an appreciation of another culture are important results of the children's years of
study of the Spanish language and culture.

In preparing for this area of study, the Spanish teacher needs to be in
close communication with the children's social studies teachers because they
share similar goals. Numerous resources available in the school and public
libraries will facilitate planning and preparation. Various books on travel
exist, from tour guides that explain travel details to photographic accounts
of travel that hint at what travelers would see. Films, maps, and pamphlets
are available. Two helpful pamphlets that list sources for travel information
are *Guide to Foreign Information Sources** and *1001 Sources for Free Travel Information.*+

The results of this study are a better understanding of people and culture in general; an understanding of a specific people and culture; an ability
to imagine oneself as a traveler to another country, enthusiasm for travel,
and an understanding of some of the facets of travel; an expansion of vocabulary and practice in dialogue and conversation; and a motivation to continue
their study and to one day take a trip like the one they have planned.

Other areas of study in Level 6 for which vocabulary has been included

---

*Chamber of Commerce of the United States, 1615 H Street N.W., Washing-
ton, DC 20006 (1974).
    +Jens Jurgen, Travel Information Bureau, P.O. Box 105, Kings Park, NY
11754 (1978).

are telling time, talking on the telephone, and eating in a restaurant. New
verbs in this level are reflexive verbs and verbs that relate to the new vocabulary. No new verb forms are taught so that verbs previously introduced
can be reviewed and used in creative ways. The basic vocabulary is listed
without verbs and modifiers since there are no new verb forms. Examples of
themes contain ideas for dramatizations and conversations.

S E L E C T I O N   A N D   U S E   O F   V O C A B U L A R Y

Los Verbos (Verb Forms)
     Three reflexive verbs are taught in previous levels: llamarse (to be
named), irse (to go away), and sentirse (to feel). In this level nine more
reflexive verbs are taught--only in the singular since they refer to personal
routines and are commonly used in the singular. The actions represented by
these verbs are good ones to pantomime and describe. Asterisk denotes the
command form of the verb.

     me acuesto, te acuestas, se acuesta (to go to bed)
     me baño, te bañas, se baña (to have a bath, bathe oneself)
     me despierto, te despiertas, se despierta (to wake up, wake oneself)
     me lavo, te lavas, se lava (to get washed, wash oneself)
     me levanto, te levantas, se levanta (to rise, get up)
     me peino, te peinas, se peina (to get combed, comb oneself)
     me pongo, te pones, se pone (to put [something] on oneself)
     me quito, te quitas, se quita (to take [something] off oneself)
     me seco, te secas, se seca (to get dried, dry oneself)

     Me acuesto a las ocho de la noche y me despierto a las ocho de la mañana.
(I go to bed at eight o'clock at night and I wake up at eight o'clock in the
morning.)
     Primero él se baña y después se peina. (First he has a bath and then he
gets combed.)
     Voy al cuarto de baño y me lavo las manos. (I go to the bathroom and I wash
my hands.)
     Me levanto temprano todos los días. (I get up early every day.)
     Me seco el pelo con una toalla grande. (I dry my hair with a big towel.)
     ¿Te pones el suéter ahora? (Are you putting on your sweater now?)
     No, me quito el suéter porque tengo calor. (No, I'm taking off my sweater
because I'm hot.)

     The other new verbs utilize the new vocabulary. They are listed here
with examples of their usage.

     contesto, contestas, contesta, contestamos, contestan, contestar (to an-
swer); llamo, llamas, llama, llamamos, llaman, llamar (to call); suena, sonar
(to ring)
     Llamo a Gloria por teléfono. (I call Gloria by telephone.)
     Juan, ¿puedes llamar a María, por favor? (John, can you call Mary, please?)
     ¿Quién quiere contestar el teléfono cuando suena? (Who wants to answer the
telephone when it rings?)

     dejo, dejas, deja, dejamos, dejan, dejar (to leave); deseo, deseas, desea,
deseamos, desean, desear (to want, desire). These verbs are used in the dramatization of eating in a restaurant.

¿Puedes dejar unas monedas para la propina? (Can you leave some coins for the tip?)
Buenos días. ¿Qué desea usted? (Good morning. What do you desire?)
Deseo dos panqueques, tocino y una taza de café. (I want two pancakes, bacon, and a cup of coffee.)

dobla,* doblar (to turn)
Voy a doblar en la próxima avenida. (I am going to turn at the next avenue.)
Dobla aquí a la derecha para ir al restaurante. (Turn here to the right in order to go to the restaurant.)

Oraciones Interrogativas (Interrogative Sentences)
Two questions introduced in this level have to do with the time of day:
¿Qué hora es? (What time is it?) ¿A qué hora (te levantas)? (What time do you [get up]?) The second question can be used with several different verbs in telling time, for example: ¿A qué hora comes el almuerzo? (What time do you eat lunch?) ¿A qué hora regresas de la escuela? (What time do you get home from school?)
Children especially enjoy being able to answer the third question: ¿Cuál es tu número de teléfono? (What is your telephone number?) It is used together with llamar (to call), contestar (to answer), and sonar (to ring) in dramatizations of talking on the telephone.

Vocabulario Suplementario (Supplementary Vocabulary)
siempre (always); temprano (early); tarde (late)
Juan siempre viene tarde. (John always comes late.)
Ellos siempre se levantan temprano. (They always get up early.)

derecho (right-hand, adj.); izquierdo (left-hand, adj.); la derecha (right side); la izquierda (left side)
Jorge tira la pelota con la mano izquierda pero María tira la pelota con la mano derecha. (George throws the ball with the left hand but Mary throws the ball with the right hand.)
Dobla a la izquierda en la esquina, después dobla a la derecha. (Turn to the left at the corner, then turn to the right.)

este (east); norte (north); oeste (west); sur (south)
Vivo al sur de la ciudad. (I live south of the city.)
¿Dónde está el norte en este mapa? (Where is north on this map?)
Voy a ir al oeste para mis vacaciones. (I am going to go to the West for my vacation.)

próximo (next, near)
Voy a comer en el próximo restaurante. (I am going to eat in the next restaurant.)

la cuenta (bill); el menú (menu); la propina (tip)
Mozo, quiero ver la cuenta, por favor. (Waiter, I want to see the bill, please.)
María, pásame el menú, por favor. (Mary, pass me the menu, please.)
Juan va a dejar la propina. (John is going to leave the tip.)

el mapa (map)
Gloria quiere ver el mapa del Perú. (Gloria wants to see the map of Peru.)

---

*Command form of the verb.

la voz (voice)
La voz de mi hermano es muy suave. (My brother's voice is very soft.)

Vocabulario Básico (Basic Vocabulary)
     Since no new verbs are introduced, the nouns alone are listed. Examples
of themes suggest ideas for separate dramatizations and conversations.

Los alimentos (Foods)

__Nouns__
la bebida   la ensalada   el postre
la comida   la fruta   la verdura

Examples of themes
Dramatizations:
A spoiled child makes life difficult for parents while eating in a restau-
   rant.
In a restaurant where it is cheaper to order the same meal for everyone in
   a group, a group tries to decide what to order.
Conversations:
Companions describe and compare what each eats throughout a typical day.
A favorite food is prepared during class time and the ingredients, measure-
   ments, and likes and dislikes in foods are discussed.

La casa (House)

__Nouns__
la bañadera   la ducha   el jabón   el peine
el cepillo   el inodoro   el lavamanos   la toalla

Examples of themes
Dramatizations:
Tourists complain to hotel manager about dirty hotel rooms.
A child wakes up late one morning and, rushing to get ready for school,
   can't find a much needed brush or comb anywhere.
Conversations:
Companions find out what each other's houses are like.
Companions describe and compare routines in getting ready for school.

La ciudad (City)

__Nouns__
la avenida   el museo   el ascensor   la esquina
la catedral   la plaza   la cuadra   en frente de
el centro   el restaurante   el edificio   la planta baja
el hotel   el teatro   la escalera   el piso
el mercado

Examples of themes
Dramatizations:
Tourists staying in an old hotel get stuck between floors on the elevator.
Two travelers are accidentally locked in a historical museum overnight and
   the statues and portraits come to life and relive the past with them.
Conversations:
Companions plan and draw a map of their town or neighborhood.

Companions describe, in order, the landmarks that each sees on the walk from home to school each day.

La comunicación (Communication)

Nouns

la llamada	la telefonista	el teléfono

Examples of themes

Dramatizations:

Salesperson tries to convince customer to buy several telephones of several colors.

A newly installed telephone malfunctions, annoying both the owners and the operator.

Conversations:

Companions describe and compare favorite television or radio programs.

Children describe and compare favorite singers.

La hora (Time)

Nouns

la hora	el reloj	el reloj de pulsera	cuarto
el minuto	el reloj despertador	el segundo	media

Examples of themes

Dramatizations:

A family who lives by the clock has life upset when all the clocks start running faster and faster.

A father takes a clock apart to show his child how it works but cannot get it back together again.

Conversations:

Companions describe and compare what each does at various hours during the day.

Children describe the kinds of watches and clocks that their families have.

La naturaleza (Nature)

Nouns

el cielo	la estrella	el mundo	la tierra
el espacio	la luna	el planeta	

Examples of themes

Dramatizations:

Children who are working inside a space ship they are building discover they are mysteriously traveling somewhere in space.

The moon falls to earth and people find that it is actually a very large and delicious pancake.

Conversations:

Children compare the geography of two Spanish speaking countries.

Companions describe and compare the landscape where each of their grandparents lives.

Los números (Numbers)

The ordinal numbers are used in ordering. They are used in the themes of other vocabulary areas.

Nouns

primero	cuarto	séptimo	décimo
segundo	quinto	octavo	
tercero	sexto	noveno	

Las profesiones (Professions)

Nouns

el astronauta	la azafata	el mozo	el piloto

Examples of themes
Dramatizations:
An astronaut lands on a new planet and finds strange creatures with unusual
  customs.
A waiter tries not to get angry with a very difficult customer.
Conversations:
Companions discuss how each prefers traveling: bus, car, train, or air-
  plane.
Children discuss which profession they want to enter and why.

El transporte (Transportation)

Nouns

la aduana	el billete	el equipaje	la maleta
el aeropuerto	el cinturón de	el horario	el pasaporte
el asiento	seguridad	la llegada	el turismo

Examples of themes
Dramatizations:
A passenger can't find a suitcase full of important papers.
A child traveling alone makes the flight unbearable for the stewardess.
Conversations:
Children discuss what they are going to pack in their suitcases on an imagi-
  nary trip to a specific Spanish speaking country.
Companions compare travel brochures for two different countries and decide
  which country each wants to visit.

V O C A B U L A R Y

Los Verbos

me acuesto	dejo	me despierto
te acuestas	dejas	te despiertas
se acuesta	deja	se despierta
me baño	dejamos	dobla*
te bañas	dejan	doblar
se baña	dejar	me lavo
contesto	deseo	te lavas
contestas	deseas	se lava
contesta	desea	me levanto
contestamos	deseamos	te levantas
contestan	desean	se levanta
contestar	desear	llamo

---

*Command form of the verb.

llamas

llama

llamamos

llaman

llamar

me peino

te peinas

se peina

me pongo

te pones

se pone

me quito

te quitas

se quita

me seco

te secas

se seca

suena

sonar

Vocabulario Básico

Los alimentos

la bebida

la comida

la ensalada

la fruta

el postre

la verdura

La casa

la bañadera

el cepillo

la ducha

el inodoro

el jabón

el lavamanos

el peine

la toalla

La ciudad

la avenida

la catedral

el centro

el hotel

el mercado

el museo

la plaza

el restaurante

el teatro

el ascensor

la cuadra

el edificio

la escalera

la esquina

en frente de

la planta baja

el piso

La comunicación

la llamada

la telefonista

el teléfono

La hora

la hora

el minuto

el reloj

el reloj despertador

el reloj de pulsera

el segundo

cuarto

media

La naturaleza

el cielo

el espacio

la estrella

la luna

el mundo

el planeta

la tierra

Los números

10,000-1,000,000

primero

segundo

tercero

cuarto

quinto

sexto

séptimo

octavo

noveno

décimo

Las profesiones

el astronauta

la azafata

el mozo

el piloto

El transporte

la aduana

el aeropuerto

el asiento

el billete

el cinturón de

seguridad

el equipaje

el horario

la llegada

la maleta

el pasaporte

el turismo

la salida

Oraciones Interrogativas

¿Qué hora es?

¿A qué hora (te levantas)?

¿Cuál es tu número de teléfono?

Vocabulario Suplementario

siempre	este	la cuenta
temprano	norte	el menú
tarde	oeste	la propina
derecho	sur	el mapa
izquierdo	próximo	la voz
la derecha		
la izquierda		

APPENDIX A

Development of Teaching Plans

The material of this curriculum is organized in outline form instead of in daily plans. The teaching plans used with a group of children should respond to their particular situation and needs. The plans should also be an expression of the teacher's own special interests, strengths, and creative ability. Therefore teaching plans need to be developed by the teachers themselves. Examples of planning are included to provide ideas.

The first plan (see Table A.1) is an example of yearly organization. It is helpful for teachers to estimate what they expect to accomplish on a monthly basis throughout the school year. A monthly plan (Table A.2) demonstrates how the material included for a particular month might be organized on a weekly basis. Suggestions for the development of daily plans and an example of a daily plan are also included.

Plans should be used as guides. Teachers should remain responsive to the children and use the plans with a certain amount of flexibility.

Daily Plans

Teachers need to give careful thought to the activities that they will include in each class period for these activities determine the success of the program. Points that need consideration in the development of the daily plan and an example of a daily plan (Table A.3) are included here. Teachers should choose formats for written plans that respond to their own needs.

1. Identifying the immediate needs of the children. The teachers determine the immediate vocabulary needs of the children based on their observations in the classroom. They consider whether the children (a) need further practice of new vocabulary, (b) are ready to combine the new vocabulary with previously learned vocabulary, (c) are ready to use the new vocabulary in creative ways, or (d) are ready for additional vocabulary words.

2. Discovering possible activities. In Levels 1-5 the Vocabulario Básico (Basic Vocabulary) contains a list of the verb forms and modifiers introduced that can be combined with the new nouns. Exploring the numerous possible combinations of these words and imagining situations in which the combinations could be used provides many ideas for activities. Teaching materials are also a source of ideas; for example, a toy house and family can suggest descriptions of the house itself, the family members, what the family members are doing, or dialogues between family members.

The children themselves are the best source of ideas for themes to be developed into dialogues and conversations. Ideas can also come from everyday

75

Table A.1. A yearly plan for Level 3: 30 minutes, 3 times a week

SEPT. (3 weeks)	OCT. (4 weeks)	NOV. (3 weeks)	DEC. (2 weeks)

Review: Previously introduced vocabulary is reviewed throughout the year.

SEPT. (3 weeks)

Los verbos
se llama
pasa
pone
saca
es*
tiene
tira
toca
ve
vive

Los colores
amarillo
anaranjado
morado

Los números
21-50

Oraciones
  interrogativas
¿De qué color
  (es la blusa)?

Vocabulario
  suplementario
él, ella
su, sus
de, del, de la

OCT. (4 weeks)

Los verbos
abre   estoy
camina   está
cierra   regresa
corre   salta
dibuja

El cuerpo
  humano
el cuello
el cuerpo
el pie
la pierna

La escuela
el bolígrafo
el borrador
el lápiz
el libro
el papel
la pizarra
el pupitre
la tiza

Expresiones
  comunes
¿Como estás?
Estoy muy bien,
  gracias.
Estoy regular,
  gracias.
¿Y tú?
Estoy muy mal.
¡Qué lástima!

Vocabulario
  suplementario
le
este, esta
aquel, aquella
aquí
allí
todo
nada
cerca de
lejos de
el dibujo

NOV. (3 weeks)

Los verbos
ama
ayuda
bebe
beber
come
comer
pasar
quiero
quiere
tengo que
tiene que

Los alimentos
el café
el chocolate
el huevo
la naranja
el panqueque
el té
el tocino

Oraciones
  interrogativas
¿Por qué (estás
  triste)?

Vocabulario
  suplementario
nadie
con
porque
feliz
triste
caliente
frío
contento
enojado
delicioso
frito

DEC. (2 weeks)

Vocabulary
introduced
this year is
reviewed and
utilized in
special
activities

---

*Verbs are listed according to the alphabetical order of the infinitive.

JAN. (3 weeks)	FEB. (3 weeks)	MAR. (3 weeks)	APR. (3 weeks)
Los verbos	Los verbos	Los verbos	Vocabulary
puedo	caminar	ayudar	introduced
puede	correr	dibujar	throughout
poner	va*	estar	this year is
sacar	regresar	lleva puesto	reviewed and
tirar	saltar	llevar puesto	utilized in
tocar	viajo		special
	viaja	El calendario	activities.
La casa	viajar	el día	
la cocina		hoy	
el comedor	Los animales	mañana	
el cuarto	el pato	la semana	
el cuarto de	el pez	lunes	
baño	la rana	martes	
el dormitorio	la tortuga	miércoles	
la sala		jueves	
	La naturaleza	viernes	
La familia	el bosque	sábado	
el bebé	el lago	domingo	
la familia	el mar		
la hermana	la montaña	La ropa	
el hermano	el valle	la bota	
los hermanos		el calcetín	
la madre	El transporte	el pijama	
el padre	el barco	la ropa	
los padres	el bote	el suéter	
		el vestido	
Vocabulario	Oraciones		
suplementario	interrogativas		
grande	¿Adónde (va Juan)?		
mediano			
pequeño	Vocabulario		
también	suplementario		
tampoco	conmigo		
	(el sábado) que		
	viene		
	el viaje		

Table A.2. A monthly plan for Level 3: January

WEEK 1	WEEK 2	WEEK 3

Review: Previously introduced vocabulary is reviewed throughout the year.

Los verbos	Los verbos	Vocabulary introduced

Los verbos	Los verbos	Vocabulary introduced this month is re- viewed and utilized in a special activi- ty, an adaptation of "Goldilocks and the Three Bears."
puedo	poner	
puede	sacar	
tocar	tirar	
La familia	**La casa**	
el bebé	la cocina	
la familia	el comedor	
la hermana	el cuarto	
el hermano	el cuarto de baño	
los hermanos	el dormitorio	
la madre	la sala	
el padre		
los padres	Vocabulario suplementario	
	grande	
Vocabulario suplementario	mediano	
también	pequeño	
tampoco		

situations in which one or more element is changed to the unexpected; for example, instead of being bothered by flies in their house, a family is bothered
by an invasion of frogs. Young children's books often develop situations of
this kind in which children delight.

  3. Developing an activity. Once an activity has been chosen it is helpful to clarify how it will be developed with the children. Introducing it
so that they understand clearly what is expected will help it begin smoothly.
This is especially important when the directions are given in Spanish. The
steps in the development will in large part be determined by the nature of the
activity itself. The activity should be concluded before the children have
grown tired of it so that when it is used again they will be eager to participate. The results of the activity need to be evaluated before planning the
next class day so that the understandings that the teacher has gained can be
used.

  4. Providing variety. It is important to vary the class activities and
routine to keep the children's interest. They should enter the classroom ea-
gerly, curious to find out what the day will bring. Change the pace of activities to help keep the children attentive; quiet activities should be followed
by active physical participation. Activities can require total group, small
group, or individual participation. The class members can be organized into
a circle, small groups, or teams. Variety in the teaching materials is also
important; the same vocabulary word can be represented with several different
kinds of materials. Songs, games, and cultural information as well as special
activities and projects need to be incorporated into the activities.

Table A.3. A daily plan for Level 3:   January, second week, second day

ACTIVITY: REVIEW OF VOCABULARY

Objectives
To review vocabulary
To encourage children
 to arrive on time
To take advantage of
 extra minutes for
 Spanish

Procedure: The activity begins when the first
children arrive; others are incorporated into it
as they come. Two piles of flash cards are
placed face down. One pile contains names of
colors; the other, animals, clothing, and foods
in random order. The children take turns drawing
two cards, one from each pile. The teacher indicates that they will use veo (I see) with the
name of the object and of the color to create a
sentence; for example: Veo la vaca morada. (I
see the purple cow.) When their sentence is correct they keep the cards; when it is not, the
cards go to the bottom of the pile.

Materials: Flash cards of previously learned vocabulary from Levels 1, 2, and 3: colors, animals, clothing, and foods

ACTIVITY: DESCRIPTIONS

Objectives
To review vocabulary
To practice the crea-
 tive use of familiar
 patterns

Procedure: With a partner, the children take
turns telling four things about a friend of
theirs; for example:

Mi amiga se llama Gloria. (My friend's name is
Gloria.)
Tiene nueve años. (She is nine years old.)
Vive en una casa amarilla. (She lives in a yel-
low house.)
Tiene dos gatos blancos y un perro negro. (She
has two white cats and a black dog.)

ACTIVITY: SONG

Objectives
To change the pace
 of the class

Procedure: A fun, active song is sung.

ACTIVITY: INTRODUCTION OF NEW VOCABULARY

Objectives
To make clear, direct
 associations between
 the objects and the
 Spanish words
To learn correct pro-
 nunciation of new
 words

Procedure: A toy dollhouse is introduced. The
teacher indicates the names of the rooms, for example, el dormitorio (bedroom), repeating the
names several times until the children pronounce
them easily and remember them.

The teacher places a toy animal, for example, el
gato (cat), in a room and models the sentence:

Table A.3. *(continued)*

To practice creating
  sentences following a
  model
To review vocabulary
To check comprehension
  of new vocabulary
To make use of new vo-
  cabulary memorable

El gato está en la cocina. (The cat is in the kitchen.) The children repeat the sentences as the animal is placed in the various rooms. The children then take turns placing the animal and stating where it is. When the children can do this easily, other familiar animals are used, for example: El caballo está en la sala. (The horse is in the living room.)

Materials: Dollhouse; toy animals from Levels 1 and 2

ACTIVITY: REVIEW OF NEW VOCABULARY

Objectives
To review body parts,
  number, sizes, and the
  verb dibuja (draw)
To create sentences using
  familiar elements

Procedure: Numbers corresponding to the number of children in the class are placed in a bag. In another bag, felt cutouts of parts of the body are placed; and in a third bag are placed flash cards with symbols for the words grande, mediano, pequeño (large or big, medium, small) that were introduced in the previous class period. The children, taking turns, secretly select a number, a body part, and a size. In numerical order, the children draw on the blackboard the body parts they have selected in the size they have select-ed. As they draw, the other children decide which body part it is and which size. When they know, they raise their hands and when called upon say, for example: Juan dibuja una boca pequeña. (John is drawing a small mouth.) Since the body parts are drawn in random order and various sizes, the children find the result humorous.

Materials: Flash cards of numbers; felt cutouts of body parts, Levels 1, 2, and 3; flash cards of large, medium, and small

ACTIVITY: FAREWELLS

Objective
To review farewells

Procedure: Each child tells the teacher good-bye with one of the farewells studied, for example:
Child: Hasta luego, Sra. López. (Until later, Mrs. Lopez.)
Teacher: Hasta luego, María. (Until later, Mary.)

APPENDIX B

The Teacher's Role

The teacher's role is discussed throughout the curriculum in relationship to the implementation of the methodology--emphasis cannot be placed too strongly on the importance of the teacher to the success of the program. The atmosphere that the teacher creates needs to be respectful and supportive of the children so that they feel secure enough to want to learn and grow. The teacher needs to develop a sensitivity to the children's feelings, a concern for them as persons, and an openness to and an appreciation of their ideas. A sense of humor is also necessary.

The children feel acceptance and respect through what their teacher says and does. A look, a smile, a touch, or just being physically close to a child are ways that the teacher can communicate a caring attitude. The teacher can demonstrate respect in the way in which the child is addressed and in what is said; commands are given politely and appreciation and praise are the rewards for good work and making an effort to do one's best.

The way in which the teacher handles the children's errors is extremely important. When children create their own sentences and dialogues and partic-ipate in conversation instead of repeating by rote, the possibility for error is much greater. Helping children develop the confidence to speak out in the second language in spite of errors is essential in teaching conversation. In-stead of criticizing the errors and censuring the children for making them, analyze the errors to determine in what areas the children need further work to clarify the grammar. The errors can be discussed with the children direct-ly if it is done in such a way that the children do not feel threatened but, rather, pleased to find ways in which they can learn to speak more correctly.

It is a good idea for the teacher to use Spanish in the classroom as much as possible so that the children become accustomed to the sounds and the flow of the language. Children like to practice understanding the Spanish from the cues of gesture and context as well as from verbal cues, and can usually de-code the general message the teacher is sending. Children rarely seek a word-for-word translation, which should be avoided in the early stages of learning a language.

The use of Spanish in the classroom should be somewhat flexible; for ex-ample, if there is a special discipline problem that is disturbing the class-room climate and the use of Spanish has not given results, the situation needs to be discussed with the child(ren) in English.

Helpful commands, directions, and questions that the teacher can use are listed here. These are key elements in the teacher's communication with the children and can be integrated with other words that the teacher uses to create a natural flow of the language. Remember that children are always addressed respectuflly, so <u>por favor</u> (please) is the first element suggested in this list.

por favor (please)	levántate (stand up, s.)
muy bien (very well)	levántense (stand up, pl.)
excelente (excellent)	mírame (look at me, s.)
repite (repeat, s.)	mírenme (look at me, pl.)
repitan (repeat, pl.)	mira hacia aquí (look over here, s.)
habla (speak, s.)	miren hacia aquí (look over here, pl.)
hablen (speak, pl.)	habla en español (speak in Spanish, s.)
cuenta (count, s.)	hablen en español (speak in Spanish, pl.)
cuenten (count, pl.)	pónganse en fila (get in line)
canten (sing, pl.)	camina (walk, s.)
más fuerte (louder)	caminen (walk, pl.)
más despacio (slower)	no corras (don't run, s.)
más rapido (faster)	no corran (don't run, pl.)
en voz alta (aloud)	espera tu turno (wait your turn, s.)
otra vez (again)	esperen sus turnos (wait your turns, pl.)
siéntate (sit down, s.)	silencio (silence)
siéntense (sit down, pl.)	

¿Quién quiere un turno ahora? (Who wants a turn now?)

¿Quién puede contar del ———— al ————? (Who can count from ———— to ————?)

¿Quién puede hacer las preguntas? (Who can make the questions?)

¿Quieres ayuda? (Do you want help?)

¿Quién puede ayudar a (Juan)? (Who can help [John]?)

APPENDIX C

Teaching Materials

The nouns listed in the basic vocabulary areas are symbols for objects in the teaching materials, which include toys, flash cards, and cutouts. The teaching materials can be purchased from various sources or prepared inexpensively. Sources for teaching materials are:

1. Donations. Parents of the children in the foreign language classes can be asked for donations of toys that are no longer used by their children. Best results come from communicating directly with the parents and explaining why the toys are needed. The children themselves can be asked to help find donations--for example, with scavanger hunts in their neighborhoods.
2. Garage sales. Toys, other objects, and children's books, whose illustrations can be used for making flash cards and paper cutouts, can be purchased inexpensively at garage sales.
3. Volunteers. Flash cards and flannel or paper cutouts can be prepared by volunteers.
4. School materials. Kindergarten teachers, speech therapists, and guidance counselors use these kinds of teaching materials; there may be a possibility of sharing materials with them.
5. Professional catalogues. Foreign language, speech therapist, and guidance counselor catalogues offer these kinds of teaching materials.
6. Toy stores.

Sturdiness, clarity, and flexibility of teaching materials is important. Since the materials will be handled on a daily basis by the children they need to be sturdy. For example, flash cards can be covered with a clear plastic adhesive paper to keep them from being soiled or easily bent. To provide clarity, materials for teaching a particular word should be only the object the word represents rather than several objects together. One way to obtain flexibility is to keep the materials from the various basic vocabulary areas in scale so that they can be used together; for example, family members, house, car, tree, and pets.

The materials need to be organized so that teachers can easily find the materials they need. It is a good idea to keep the materials for a particular level together. Flash cards can be separated by levels in a file box. If several classes of the same level meet at the same time of day, it may be necessary to have duplicates of some of the materials.

APPENDIX D
Vocabulary

L O S   V E R B O S   (V E R B S)

Infinitive	Level 1	Level 2	Level 3	Level 4	Level 5	Level 6
abrir (to open)		abre* abro	abre	abres+ abrir	abrimos abren	
acostarse (to go to bed)						me acuesto te acuestas se acuesta
amar (to love)		amo	ama			
ayudar (to help)		ayudo	ayuda ayudar	ayudas	ayudamos ayudan	
bañarse (to have a bath, bathe oneself)						me baño te bañas se baña
beber (to drink)		bebo	bebe beber	bebes	bebemos beben	
caminar (to walk)		camina* camino	camina caminar	caminas	caminamos caminan	
cerrar (to close)		cierra* cierro	cierra	cierras cerrar	cerramos cierran	
comer (to eat)		como	come comer	comes	comemos comen	
comprar (to buy)					compro compras compra compramos compran comprar	
contestar (to answer)						contesto contestas contesta contestamos contestan contestar

*Command form of the verb.
+Each verb given in the second person intimate is also taught in the second person formal.

85

Infinitive	Level 1	Level 2	Level 3	Level 4	Level 5	Level 6
correr (to run)		corre* corro	corre correr	corres	corremos corren	
costar (to cost)					cuesta cuestan	
dejar (to leave)						dejo dejas deja dejamos dejan dejar
desear (to want, desire)						deseo deseas desea deseamos desean desear
despertarse (to wake up, wake oneself)						me despierto te despiertas se despierta
dibujar (to draw)		dibuja* dibujo	dibuja dibujar	dibujas	dibujamos dibujan	
doblar (to turn)						dobla* doblar
doler (to hurt)		duele duelen				
dormir (to sleep)					duermo duermes duerme dormimos duermen dormir	
entender (to understand, to comprehend)				entiendo entiendes entiende entender	entendemos entienden	

Verb				
escuchar (to listen to, to hear)	escucho escuchas escucha escuchar			escuchamos escuchan
estar (to be)	estás	estoy está estar		estamos están
estudiar (to study)	estudio estudias estudia estudiar			estudiamos estudian
gustar (to please)			gusta gustan	
haber (there to be)			hay	
hablar (to speak, to talk)	hablo hablas habla hablar			hablamos hablan
hacer (to do)	hace			hago haces hacemos hacen hacer
ir (to go)	vas ir	va	voy	vamos van
irse (to go away)	me voy te vas se va irse			nos vamos se van
jugar (to play)	juego juegas juega jugar			jugamos juegan
lavar (to wash)	lavo lavas lava lavar			lavamos lavan

---

*Command form of the verb.

87

Infinitive	Level 1	Level 2	Level 3	Level 4	Level 5	Level 6
lavarse (to get washed, wash oneself)						me lavo / te lavas / se lava
levantarse (to rise, get up)						me levanto / te levantas / se levanta
llamar (to call)						llamo / llamas / llama / llamamos / llaman / llamar
llamarse (to be named)	me llamo		se llama	te llamas	nos llamamos / se llaman	
llevar (to carry, to take)				llevo / llevas / lleva / llevar	llevamos / llevan	
llevar puesto (to wear)		llevo puesto	lleva puesto / llevar puesto	llevas puesto	llevamos puesto / llevan puestos	
llover (to rain)				llueve / llover		
mirar (to look at, watch)					miro / miras / mira / miramos / miran / mirar	
nevar (to snow)				nieva / nevar		
pagar (to pay)					pago / pagas / paga / pagamos / pagan / pagar	

Infinitive	Command*					Reflexive
pasar (to pass)	pásame*	paso	pasa / pasar	pasas	pasamos / pasan	
peinarse (to get combed, comb oneself)						me peino / te peinas / se peina
poder (to be able [to])			puedo / puede	puedes / poder	podemos / pueden	
poner (to put on)	pon*	pongo	pone / poner	pones	ponemos / ponen	
ponerse (to put [something] on oneself)						me pongo / te pones / se pone
preparar (to prepare)				preparo / preparas / prepara / preparar	preparamos / preparan	
querer (to want)			quiero / quiere	quieres / querer	queremos / quieren	
quitarse (to take [something] off oneself)						me quito / te quitas / se quita
regresar (to return)		regreso	regresa / regresar	regresas	regresamos / regresan	
sacar (to remove)	saca*	saco	saca / sacar	sacas	sacamos / sacan	
saltar (to jump)		salta* / salto	salta / saltar	saltas	saltamos / saltan	
secarse (to get dried, dry oneself)						me seco / te secas / se seca
sentirse (to feel)				me siento / te sientes / se siente	nos sentimos / se sienten	
ser (to be)		soy	es	eres / ser	somos / son	

89

---

*Command form of the verb.

Infinitive	Level 1	Level 2	Level 3	Level 4	Level 5	Level 6
sonar (to ring)						suena sonar
tener (to have)		tengo	tiene	tienes tener	tenemos tienen	
tener que (to have to)			tengo que tiene que	tienes que tener que	tenemos que tienen que	
tirar (to throw)	tiráme*	tiro	tira tirar	tiras	tiramos tiran	
tocar (to touch)	toca*	toco	toca tocar	tocas	tocamos tocan	
vender (to sell)					vendo vendes vende vendemos venden vender	
venir (to come)				vengo vienes viene venir	venimos vienen	
ver (to see)		veo	ve	ves ver	vemos ven	
viajar (to travel)			viajo viaja viajar	viajas	viajamos viajan	
visitar (to visit)				visito visitas visita visitar	visitamos visitan	
vivir (to live)	vivo		vive	vives vivir	vivimos viven	

*Command form of the verb.

V O C A B U L A R I O   B Á S I C O   (B A S I C   V O C A B U L A R Y)

Level 1	Level 2	Level 3	Level 4	Level 5	Level 6

Los alimentos (Foods)

Level 1	Level 2	Level 3	Level 4	Level 5	Level 6
la manzana (apple)	el agua (water)	el café (coffee)	el almuerzo (lunch)	la carne de vaca (beef)	la bebida (beverage)
la piña (pineapple)	el azúcar (sugar)	el chocolate (cocoa)	el dulce (candy)	la cena (supper)	la comida (food)
el plátano (banana)	el cereal (cereal)	el huevo (egg)	la gelatina (gelatin)	el flan (custard)	la ensalada (salad)
	el desayuno (breakfast)	la naranja (orange)	la hamburguesa (hamburger)	la lechuga (lettuce)	la fruta (fruit)
	el jugo (juice)	el panqueque (pancake)	el helado (ice cream)	el maíz (corn)	el postre (dessert)
	la leche (milk)	el té (tea)	la papa (potato)	el melón (melon)	la verdura (vegetable)
	el pan (bread)	el tocino (bacon)	las papas fritas (french fries)	el pescado (fish)	
	la tostada (toast)		el perro caliente (hot dog)	el pollo (chicken)	
			el sandwich (sandwich)	el tomate (tomato)	
			la sopa (soup)	la torta (cake)	
				las uvas (grapes)	
				la zanahoria (carrot)	

Los animales (Animals)

Level 1	Level 2	Level 3	Level 4	Level 5	Level 6
el gato (cat)	el animal (animal)	el pato (duck)	el camello (camel)	la ardilla (squirrel)	
el perro (dog)	el caballo (horse)	el pez (fish)	el elefante (elephant)	el ciervo (deer)	
	el cerdo (pig)	la rana (frog)	la girafa (giraffe)	el conejo (rabbit)	
	la gallina (hen)	la tortuga (turtle)	el hipopótamo (hippopotamus)	el lobo (wolf)	

Level 1	Level 2	Level 3	Level 4	Level 5	Level 6

Los animales (Animals) (continued)

Level 1	Level 2	Level 3	Level 4	Level 5	Level 6
	la oveja (sheep)		el león (lion)	el oso (bear)	
	la vaca (cow)		el mono (monkey)	el pájaro (bird)	
			el tigre (tiger)	la serpiente (snake)	
				el zorro (fox)	

El calendario (Calendar)

Level 1	Level 2	Level 3	Level 4	Level 5	Level 6
		el día (day)	el año (year)	la fecha (date)	
		hoy (today)	la estación (season)	el mes (month)	
		mañana (tomorrow)	la primavera (spring)	enero (January)	
		la semana (week)	el verano (summer)	febrero (February)	
		lunes (Monday)	el otoño (autumn)	marzo (March)	
		martes (Tuesday)	el invierno (winter)	abril (April)	
		miércoles (Wednesday)		mayo (May)	
		jueves (Thursday)		junio (June)	
		viernes (Friday)		julio (July)	
		sábado (Saturday)		agosto (August)	
		domingo (Sunday)		septiembre (September)	
				octubre (October)	

noviembre (November)
diciembre (December)

La casa (House)

la casa (house)
el garaje (garage)
la puerta (door)
la ventana (window)

la cocina (kitchen)
el comedor (dining room)
el cuarto (room)
el cuarto de baño (bathroom)
el dormitorio (bedroom)
la sala (living room)

la cuchara (spoon)
el cuchillo (knife)
el horno (stove)
la mesa (table)
el plato (dish)
el refrigerador (refrigerator)
la silla (chair)
la taza (cup)
el tenedor (fork)
el vaso (glass)

la alfombra (rug)
la almohada (pillow)
la cama (bed)
la cómoda (commode)
el espejo (mirror)
la frazada (blanket)
la lámpara (lamp)
la luz (light)
el sillón (arm-chair)
el sofá (sofa)

la bañadera (bathtub)
el cepillo (brush)
la ducha (shower)
el inodoro (toilet)
el jabón (soap)
el lavamanos (wash-stand)
el peine (comb)
la toalla (towel)

La ciudad (City)

la acera (sidewalk)
la calle (street)
la ciudad (city)
el jardín zoológico (zoo)
el parque (park)

el cine (cinema)
el hospital (hospital)
la iglesia (church)
el supermercado (supermarket)
la tienda (shop)

la avenida (avenue)
la catedral (cathedral)
el centro (center)
el hotel (hotel)
el mercado (market)

Level 1	Level 2	Level 3	Level 4	Level 5	Level 6

La ciudad (City) (continued)

			Level 4	Level 5	Level 6
			el pueblo (town)		el museo (museum) la plaza (square) el restaurante (restaurant) el teatro (theater) el ascensor (elevator) la cuadra (block) el edificio (building) la escalera (stairs) la esquina (corner) en frente de (opposite) la planta baja (first floor) el piso (floor)

El clima (Climate)

			Level 4	Level 5	Level 6
			(hace) calor (it is hot) (hace) fresco (it is cool) (hace) frío (it is cold) la lluvia (rain)	el hielo (ice) la nube (cloud) la tormenta (storm) el viento (wind)	

94

la nieve (snow)
el sol (sun)
el tiempo (weather)

La comunicación (Communication)

el disco (record)
la música (music)
las noticias (news)
el programa (program)
la propaganda (advertising)
el radio (radio)
la televisión (television)
el televisor (television set)
el tocadiscos (record player)
la llamada (call)
la telefonista (operator)
el teléfono (telephone)

Los colores (Colors)

el color (color)
blanco (white)
negro (black)
rojo (red)

azul (blue)
marrón (brown)
verde (green)

amarillo (yellow)
anaranjado (orange)
morado (purple)

azul celeste (light blue)
gris (grey)
rosado (pink)

95

El cuerpo humano (Body parts)

Level 1	Level 2	Level 3	Level 4	Level 5	Level 6
la boca (mouth)	el brazo (arm)	el cuello (neck)	la espalda (back)		
la cabeza (head)	la cara (face)	el cuerpo (body)	el diente (tooth)		
la mano (hand)	el dedo (finger)	el pie (foot)	la garganta (throat)		
la nariz (nose)	la lengua (tongue)	la pierna (leg)	el vientre (stomach)		
el ojo (eye)	la oreja (ear)				
el pelo (hair)					

La escuela (School)

Level 1	Level 2	Level 3	Level 4	Level 5	Level 6
	la alumna (student, f.)	el bolígrafo (pen)	la clase (class)		
	el alumno (student, m.)	el borrador (eraser)	el grado (grade)		
	el aula (classroom)	el lápiz (pencil)	el timbre (bell)		
	la escuela (school)	el libro (book)			
	el profesor (teacher, m.)	el papel (paper)			
	la profesora (teacher, f.)	la pizarra (blackboard)			
		el pupitre (desk)			
		la tiza (chalk)			

La familia (Family)

Level 1	Level 2	Level 3	Level 4	Level 5	Level 6
la mamá (mom)	la abuela (grandmother)	el bebé (baby)	la hija (daughter)	la prima (cousin, f.)	
la niña (girl)	el abuelo (grandfather)	la familia (family)	el hijo (son)	el primo (cousin, m.)	

el niño (boy)
el papá (dad)

los abuelos (grandparents)

la hermana (sister)
el hermano (brother)
los hermanos (brothers and sisters)
la madre (mother)
el padre (father)
los padres (parents)

la tía (aunt)
el tío (uncle)

La hora (Time)

la mañana (morning)
la noche (night)
la tarde (afternoon)

la hora (hour, time)
el minuto (minute)
el reloj (clock)
el reloj despertador (alarm clock)
el reloj de pulsera (wrist watch)
el segundo (second)
cuarto (quarter)
media (half)

La naturaleza (Nature)

el árbol (tree)
la flor (flower)

el bosque (woods)
el lago (lake)
el mar (sea)

la arena (sand)
el barro (mud)
el desierto (desert)

el cielo (sky)
el espacio (space)
la estrella (star)

Level 1	Level 2	Level 3	Level 4	Level 5	Level 6

La naturaleza (Nature) (continued)

Level 1	Level 2	Level 3	Level 4	Level 5	Level 6
		la montaña (mountain) el valle (valley)	la playa (beach) el río (river) la selva (jungle)		la luna (moon) el mundo (world) el planeta (planet) la tierra (earth)

Los números (Numbers)

Level 1	Level 2	Level 3	Level 4	Level 5	Level 6
el número (number) 1-10	11-20	21-50	51-100	101-10,000	10,000-1,000,000 primero (first) segundo (second) tercero (third) cuarto (fourth) quinto (fifth) sexto (sixth) séptimo (seventh) octavo (eighth) noveno (ninth) décimo (tenth)

Las profesiones (Professions)

Level 1	Level 2	Level 3	Level 4	Level 5	Level 6
			el dentista (dentist)	el anunciador (announcer)	el astronauta (astronaut)

el enfermero (nurse)
el médico (doctor)
el paciente (patient)
el policía (policeman)

el cantante (singer)
el dependiente (clerk)
el reportero (newscaster)

la azafata (stewardess)
el mozo (waiter)
el piloto (pilot)

La ropa (Clothing)

la blusa (blouse)
la camisa (shirt)
la falda (skirt)
los pantalones (pants)
el zapato (shoe)

la bota (boot)
el calcetín (sock)
el pijama (pajamas)
la ropa (clothing)
el suéter (sweater)
el vestido (dress)

la bufanda (scarf)
la chaqueta (jacket)
el gorro (cap)
el guante (glove)
el impermeable (raincoat)
el paraguas (umbrella)
el sombrero (hat)

la bolsa (bag)
la cartera (purse)
el cinturón (belt)
las gafas (eyeglasses)
la talla (size)

El transporte (Transportation)

el automóvil (car)
el avión (airplane)

la bicicleta (bicycle)
el tractor (tractor)

el barco (ship)
el bote (boat)

el autobús (bus)
el taxi (taxi)
el tren (train)

la aduana (customs)
el aeropuerto (airport)
el asiento (seat)
el billete (ticket)
el cinturón de seguridad (safety belt)

99

Level 1	Level 2	Level 3	Level 4	Level 5	Level 6

El transporte (Transportation)(continued)

Level 1	Level 2	Level 3	Level 4	Level 5	Level 6
					el equipaje (luggage)
					el horario (schedule)
					la llegada (arrival)
					la maleta (suitcase)
					el pasaporte (passport)
					el turismo (tourism)
					la salida (departure)

ORACIONES INTERROGATIVAS (INTERROGATIVE SENTENCES)

Level 1	Level 2	Level 3	Level 4	Level 5	Level 6
¿Cómo te llamas? (What is your name?)	¿Cuántos años tienes? (How old are you?)	¿Adónde (va Juan)? (Where [is John going]?)	¿Cuál es (tu dirección)? (What is [your address]?)	¿Cuánto cuesta (la cartera)? (How much is [the purse]?)	¿Qué hora es? (What time is it?)
¿Dónde vives? (Where do you live?)	¿Cuántos ———— hay? (How many are there?)	¿De qué color (es la blusa)? (What color [is the blouse]?)	¿Cuándo (te vas de vacaciones)? (When [do you go away on vacation]?)	¿De qué talla es (el vestido)? (What size is [the dress]?)	¿A qué hora (te levantas)? (What time do you [get up]?)
	¿Qué ves? (What do you see?)	¿Por qué (estás triste)? (Why [are you sad]?)		¿Cuál es la fecha? (What is the date?)	¿Cuál es tu número de teléfono? (What is your telephone number?)
	¿Dónde te duele? (Where do you hurt?)				

EXPRESIONES COMUNES (COMMON EXPRESSIONS)

Level 1	Level 2	Level 3	Level 4	Level 5	Level 6
adiós (good-bye)	buenas noches (good night)	¿Cómo estás? (How are you?)	¿Cómo está usted? (How are you?)		
buenos días (good morning)	buenas tardes (good afternoon)	Estoy muy bien, gracias. (I am very well, thank you.)	Me siento (mejor). (I feel [better].)		
de nada (you're welcome)	hasta luego (until later)	Estoy regular, gracias. (I am not bad, thank you.)	¡Hola! (Hi!)		
gracias (thank you)		¿Y tú? (And you?)	¿Qué tal? (How are you?)		
perdón (pardon)		Estoy muy mal. (I am very sick.)	¡Qué lluvia tan fuerte! (What a heavy rain!)		
por favor (please)		¡Qué lástima! (What a pity!)	¡Qué animal feroz! (What a ferocious animal!)		
repite (repeat)					

101

VOCABULARIO SUPLEMENTARIO (SUPPLEMENTARY VOCABULARY)

Level 1
- en (in)
- señor (Mr.)
- señora (Mrs.)
- señorita (Miss)
- la pelota (ball)

Level 2
- yo (I, subject pronoun)
- mi, mis (my--s., pl.)
- me (to me)
- mí (me)
- un, una (a, an--m., f.)
- unos, unas (some--m., f.)
- a, al, a la (to)
- sí (yes)
- no (no)
- y (and)
- o (either, or)
- ni (neither, nor)
- pero (but)
- rápidamente (rapidly)
- lentamente (slowly)
- muy (very)
- más (more)

Level 3
- él, ella (he, she--subject; him, her--object of preposition)
- su, sus (his, her)
- le (to him, to her)
- nadie (nobody)
- de, del, de la (of, from, to)
- este, esta (this--m.,f.)
- aquel, aquella (that--m., f.)
- aquí (here)
- allí (there)
- con (with)
- conmigo (with me)
- también (also, too)
- tampoco (neither, not either)
- todo (all, every)
- nada (nothing, not anything)

Level 4
- tú (you--int.)
- usted (you--for.)
- tu, tus (your--int.)
- su, sus (your--for.)
- te (to you--int.)
- le (to you--int.)
- tí (to you--for.)
- contigo (you)
- sí (with you--int.)
- si (if)
- cuando (when)
- mientras (que) (while)
- por (during, for; in; through, along)
- para (destined for; to be used for)
- todavía (still, yet)
- ya (already; now, at once)

Level 5
- nosotros, nosotras (we--m. f., subject; us, object of preposition)
- ustedes (you--subject, object of preposition)
- ellos, ellas (they--m., f., subject; them, object of preposition)
- nuestro, nuestros (our--m.)
- nuestra, nuestras (our--f.)
- su, sus (your, their)
- nos (to us)
- les (to you)
- alto (tall)
- bajo (short)
- rico (rich)
- pobre (poor)
- caro (expensive)
- barato (cheap)

Level 6
- siempre (always)
- temprano (early)
- tarde (late)
- derecho (right-hand, adj.)
- izquierdo (left-hand, adj.)
- la derecha (right side)
- la izquierda (left side)
- norte (north)
- sur (south)
- este (east)
- oeste (west)
- próximo (next, near)
- la cuenta (bill)
- el menú (menu)
- la propina (tip)
- el mapa (map)

menos (less)
ahora (now)
después (after, later, next)
hacia (toward)
abierto (open)
cerrado (closed)
bonito (pretty)
feo (ugly)
nuevo (new)
viejo (old)
limpio (clean)
sucio (dirty)
mucho (a lot of)
poco (little)
(tengo) calor (I'm hot)
(tengo) frío (I'm cold)
(tengo) hambre (I'm hungry)
(tengo) sed (I'm thirsty)

porque (because)
el sábado que viene
viene (next Saturday)
cerca de (close to)
lejos de (far from)
feliz (happy)
triste (sad)
caliente (hot)
frío (cold)
contento (content)
enojado (angry)
delicioso (delicious)
frito (fried)
grande (large, big)
mediano (medium)
pequeño (small)
el dibujo (drawing)
el viaje (trip)

seco (dry)
mojado (wet)
roto (broken)
sano (sound)
manso (tame, gentle)
feroz (savage, ferocious)
fuerte (hard, strong)
suave (soft, gentle)
mejor (better)
peor (worse)
(tener) miedo (to be frightened)
(el) inglés (English)
(el) español (Spanish)
las vacaciones (vacation)
la visita (visit, visitor)

enfermo (sick)
sano (healthy)
apagado (turned off)
encendido (turned on)
rebajado (reduced, lowered)
aumentado (increased, raised)
demasiado (too--followed by an adjective or adverb; too much-- s., too many--pl.)
suficiente (sufficient, enough)
juntos (together)
el cambio (change)
el dinero (money)
la moneda (coin)
el paquete (package)
el precio (price)
(ir de) compras (to go shopping)
(hacer) compras (to do the shopping)

la voz (voice)

103

Level 1	Level 2	Level 3	Level 4	Level 5	Level 6
	(tengo) sueño (I'm sleepy)			el dolor (pain)	
	la amiga (friend--f.)			la gripe (flu)	
	el amigo (friend--m.)			la medicina (medicine)	
	el cumpleaños (birthday)			el resfriado (cold)	
	la granja (farm)				

Index